Date Due

" Of what is't fools make such vain keeping?
Sin their conception, their birth weeping,
Their life a general mist of error,
Their death a hideous storm of terror."

The contempt of the world is the chief theme of
edification. A charnel filled with festering corpses,
snakes, and worms points the preacher's moral.
Before the eyes of all, in terror-stricken vision or in
nightmares of uneasy conscience, leap the inextinguish-
able flames of hell. Salvation, meanwhile, is being
sought through amulets, relics, pilgrimages to holy
places, fetishes of divers sorts and different degrees
of potency. The faculties of the heart and head,
defrauded of wholesome sustenance, have recourse to
delirious debauches of the fancy, dreams of magic,
compacts with the evil one, insanities of desire, inepti-
tudes of discipline. Sexual passion, ignoring the true
place of woman in society, treats her on the one hand
like a servile instrument, on the other exalts her to
sainthood or execrates her as the chief impediment to
holiness. Common sense, sanity of judgment, acceptance of things as they are, resolution to ameliorate the
evils and to utilise the goods of life, seem everywhere
deficient. Men are obstinate in misconception of their
proper aims, wasting their energies upon shadows instead

of holding fast by realities, waiting for a future whereof they know nothing, in lieu of mastering and economising the present. The largest and most serious undertakings of united Europe in this period—the Crusades —are based upon a radical mistake. " Why seek ye the living among the dead ? Behold, He is not here, but risen ! " With these words ringing in their ears, the nations flock to Palestine and pour their blood forth for an empty sepulchre. The one Emperor who attains the object of Christendom by rational means is excommunicated for his success. Frederick II. returns from the Holy Land a ruined man because he made a compact useful to his Christian subjects with the Chief of Islam.

II

Such are some of the stereotyped ideas which crowd our mind when we reflect upon the Middle Ages. They are certainly one-sided. Drawn for the most part from the study of monastic literature, exaggerated by that reaction against medievalism which the Renaissance initiated, they must be regarded as inadequate to represent the whole truth. At no one period between

THE MEDIEVAL LIBRARY UNDER
THE GENERAL EDITORSHIP OF
SIR ISRAEL GOLLANCZ, Litt.D., F.B.A.

WINE, WOMEN, AND SONG

"THE TAVERN'S PLEASURES"

*Reproduced from the "Navis Stultifera" of Sebastian Brandt,
first Latin edition, 1497*

WINE
WOMEN AND SONG

MEDIÆVAL LATIN STUDENTS'
SONGS NOW FIRST TRANSLATED
INTO ENGLISH VERSE WITH AN
ESSAY BY JOHN ADDINGTON
SYMONDS

COOPER SQUARE PUBLISHERS, INC.
NEW YORK
1966

"WER LIEBT NICHT WEIB WEIN UND GESANG
DER BLEIBT EIN NARR SEIN LEBENSLANG."

Martin Luther.

80929

Published 1966 by Cooper Square Publishers, Inc.
59 Fourth Avenue, New York, N. Y. 10003
Library of Congress Catalog Card No. 66-26826

Printed in the United States of America
by Noble Offset Printers Inc., New York, N. Y. 10003

TO

ROBERT LOUIS STEVENSON

DEAR LOUIS,

To you, in memory of past symposia, when wit (your wit) flowed freer than our old Forzato, I dedicate this little book, my pastime through three anxious months.

Yours,

JOHN ADDINGTON SYMONDS.

Villa Emily, San Remo
May 1884.

CONTENTS

CONTENTS

WINE, WOMEN, AND SONG

I

WHEN we try to picture to ourselves the intellectual and moral state of Europe in the Middle Ages, some fixed and almost stereotyped ideas immediately suggest themselves. We think of the nations immersed in a gross mental lethargy; passively witnessing the gradual extinction of arts and sciences which Greece and Rome had splendidly inaugurated; allowing libraries and monuments of antique civilisation to crumble into dust; while they trembled under a dull and brooding terror of coming judgment, shrank from natural enjoyment as from deadly sin, or yielded themselves with brutal eagerness to the satisfaction of vulgar appetites. Preoccupation with the other world in this long period weakens man's hold upon the things that make his life desirable. Philosophy is sunk in the slough of ignorant, perversely subtle disputation upon subjects destitute of actuality. Theological fanaticism has extinguished liberal studies and the gropings of the reason after truth in positive experience. Society lies prostrate under the heel of tyrannous orthodoxy. We discern men in masses, aggregations, classes, guilds— everywhere the genus and the species of humanity, rarely and by luminous exception individuals and persons. Universal ideals of Church and Empire clog and confuse the nascent nationalities. Prolonged habits of extra-mundane contemplation, combined with the decay of real knowledge, volatilise the thoughts and aspirations of the best and wisest into dreamy un-realities, giving a false air of mysticism to love, shroud-ing art in allegory, reducing the interpretation of texts to an exercise of idle ingenuity, and the study of Nature (in Bestiaries, Lapidaries, and the like) to an insane system of grotesque and pious quibbling. The conception of man's fall and of the incurable badness of this world bears poisonous fruit of cynicism and asceticism, that twofold bitter almond hidden in the harsh monastic shell. The devil has become God upon this earth, and God's eternal jailer in the next world. Nature is regarded with suspicion and aver-sion; the flesh, with shame and loathing, broken by spasmodic outbursts of lawless self-indulgence. For human life there is one formula :—

the fall of the Roman Empire and the close of the thirteenth century was the mental atmosphere of Europe so unnaturally clouded. Yet there is sufficient substance in them to justify their formulation. The earlier Middle Ages did, in fact, extinguish antique civility. The later Middle Ages did create, to use a phrase of Michelet, an army of dunces for the maintenance of orthodoxy. The intellect and the conscience became used to moving paralytically among visions, dreams, and mystic terrors, weighed down with torpor, abusing virile faculties for the suppression of truth and the perpetuation of revered error.

It is, therefore, with a sense of surprise, with something like a shock to preconceived opinions, that we first become acquainted with the medieval literature which it is my object in the present treatise to make better known to English readers. That so bold, so fresh, so natural, so pagan a view of human life as the Latin songs of the Wandering Students exhibit, should have found clear and artistic utterance in the epoch of the Crusades, is indeed enough to bid us pause and reconsider the justice of our stereotyped ideas about that period. This literature makes it manifest that the ineradicable appetites and natural instincts of men and women were no less vigorous in fact, though less articu-

late and self-assertive, than they had been in the age of
Greece and Rome, and than they afterwards displayed
themselves in what is known as the Renaissance.

With something of the same kind we have long been
familiar in the Troubadour poetry of Provence. But
Provençal literature has a strong chivalrous tincture,
and every one is aware with what relentless fury the
civilisation which produced it was stamped out by the
Church. The literature of the Wandering Students,
on the other hand, owes nothing to chivalry, and
emanates from a class which formed a subordinate part
of the ecclesiastical militia. It is almost vulgar in its
presentment of common human impulses ; it bears the
mark of the proletariate, though adorned with flourishes
betokening the neighbourhood of Church and University.

III

Much has recently been written upon the subject
of an abortive Renaissance within the Middle Ages.
The centre of it was France, and its period of brilliancy
may be roughly defined as the middle and end of the
twelfth century. Much, again, has been said about
the religious movement in England, which spread to

Eastern Europe, and anticipated the Reformation by two centuries before the date of Luther. The songs of the Wandering Students, composed for the most part in the twelfth century, illustrate both of these early efforts after self-emancipation. Uttering the unrestrained emotions of men attached by a slender tie to the dominant clerical class and diffused over all countries, they bring us face to face with a body of opinion which finds in studied chronicle or laboured dissertation of the period no echo. On the one side, they express that delight in life and physical enjoyment which was a main characteristic of the Renaissance; on the other, they proclaim that revolt against the corruption of Papal Rome which was the motive-force of the Reformation.

Our knowledge of this poetry is derived from two chief sources. One is a MS. of the thirteenth century, which was long preserved in the monastery of Benedict-beuern in Upper Bavaria, and is now at Munich. Richly illuminated with rare and curious illustrations of contemporary manners, it seems to have been compiled for the use of some ecclesiastical prince. This fine codex was edited in 1847 at Stuttgart. The title of the publication is *Carmina Burana*, and under that designation I shall refer to it. The other is a Harleian MS., written before 1264, which Mr. Thomas Wright collated with other English MSS., and published in 1841 under the name of *Latin Poems commonly attributed to Walter Mapes.*

These two sources have to some extent a common stock of poems, which proves the wide diffusion of the songs in question before the date assignable to the earlier of the two MS. authorities. But while this is so, it must be observed that the *Carmina Burana* are richer in compositions which form a prelude to the Renaissance; the English collections, on the other hand, contain a larger number of serious and satirical pieces anticipating the Reformation.

Another important set of documents for the study of the subject are the three large works of Edelstand du Méril upon popular Latin poetry; while the stores at our disposal have been otherwise augmented by occasional publications of German and English scholars, bringing to light numerous scattered specimens of a like description. Of late it has been the fashion in Germany to multiply anthologies of medieval student-songs, intended for companion volumes to the *Commersbuch*. Among these, one entitled *Gaudeamus* (Teubner, 2d edition, 1879) deserves honourable mention.

It is my purpose to give a short account of what is known about the authors of these verses, to analyse the general characteristics of their art, and to illustrate the theme by copious translations.   So far as I am aware, the songs of Wandering Students offer almost absolutely untrodden ground to the English translator; and this fact may be pleaded in excuse for the large number which I have laid under contribution.

In carrying out my plan, I shall confine myself principally, but not strictly, to the *Carmina Burana*. I wish to keep in view the anticipation of the Renaissance rather than to dwell upon those elements which indicate an early desire for ecclesiastical reform.

IV

We have reason to conjecture that the Romans, even during the classical period of their literature, used accentual rhythms for popular poetry, while quantitative metres formed upon Greek models were the artificial modes employed by cultivated writers. However this may be, there is no doubt that, together with the decline of antique civilisation, accent and rhythm began to displace quantity and metre in Latin versification. Quantitative measures, like the Sapphic and Hexameter, were composed accentually. The services and music of the Church introduced new systems of prosody. Rhymes, both single and double, were added to the verse ; and the extraordinary flexibility of medieval Latin—that sonorous instrument of varied rhetoric used by Augustine in the prose of the *Confessions,* and gifted with poetic inspiration in such hymns as the *Dies Irae* or the *Stabat Mater*—rendered this new vehicle of literary utterance adequate to all the tasks imposed on it by piety and metaphysic. The language of the *Confessions* and the *Dies Irae* is not, in fact, a decadent form of Cicero's prose or Virgil's verse, but a development of the Roman speech in accordance with the new conditions introduced by Christianity. It remained comparatively sterile in the department of prose composition, but it attained to high qualities of art in the verse and rhythms of men like Thomas of Celano, Thomas of Aquino, Adam of St. Victor, Bernard of Morlais, and Bernard of Clairvaux. At the same time, classical Latin literature continued to be languidly studied in the cloisters and the schools of grammar. The metres of the ancients were practised with uncouth and patient assiduity, strenuous efforts being made to keep alive an art which was no

longer rightly understood.   Rhyme invaded the hexameter, and the best verses of the medieval period in
that measure were leonine.

The hymns of the Church and the secular songs
composed for music in this base Latin took a great
variety of rhythmic forms.   It is clear that vocal
melody controlled their movement; and one fixed
element in all these compositions was rhyme—rhyme
often intricate and complex beyond hope of imitation
in our language.   Elision came to be disregarded;
and even the accentual values, which may at first
have formed a substitute for quantity, yielded to musical notation.   The epithet of popular belongs to these
songs in a very real sense, since they were intended
for the people's use, and sprang from popular emotion.
Poems of this class were technically known as *moduli*—
a name which points significantly to the importance of
music in their structure.   Imitations of Ovid's elegiacs
or of Virgil's hexameters obtained the name of *versus*.
Thus Walter of Lille, the author of a regular epic
poem on Alexander, one of the best medieval writers
of *versus*, celebrates his skill in the other department
of popular poetry thus—

> "Perstrepuit *modulis* Gallia tota meis."
> (All France rang with my songs.)

We might compare the *versus* of the Middle Ages with the stiff sculptures on a Romanesque font, lifelessly reminiscent of decadent classical art; while the *moduli*, in their freshness, elasticity, and vigour of invention, resemble the floral scrolls, foliated cusps, and grotesque basreliefs of Gothic or Lombard architecture.

V

Even in the half-light of what used to be called emphatically the Dark Ages, there pierce gleams which may be reflections from the past evening of paganism, or may intimate the earliest dawn of modern times.   One of these is a song, partly popular, partly scholastic, addressed to a beautiful boy.[1]   It begins thus—

> "O admirabile veneris idŏlum"—

and continues in this strain, upon the same rhythm, blending reminiscences of classical mythology and medieval metaphysic, and winding up with a reference

[1] Du Méril, *Poésies Populaires Latines Antérieures au Deuxième Siècle*, p. 240.

to the Horatian *Vitas hinnuleo me similis Chloe.* This poem was composed in the seventh century, probably at Verona, for mention is made in it of the river Adige. The metre can perhaps be regarded as a barbarous treatment of the long Asclepiad; but each line seems to work out into two bars, divided by a marked rest, with two accents to each bar, and shows by what sort of transition the modern French Alexandrine may have been developed.

The oddly archaic phraseology of this love-song rendered it unfit for translation; but I have tried my hand at a kind of hymn in praise of Rome, which is written in the same peculiar rhythm:[1] —

"O Rome illustrious, of the world emperess!
 Over all cities thou queen in thy goodliness!
 Red with the roseate blood of the martyrs, and
 White with the lilies of virgins at God's right hand!
 Welcome we sing to thee; ever we bring to thee
 Blessings, and pay to thee praise for eternity.

 Peter, thou praepotent warder of Paradise,
 Hear thou with mildness the prayer of thy votaries;
 When thou art seated to judge the twelve tribes, O then
 Show thyself merciful; be thou benign to men;
 And when we call to thee now in the world's distress,
 Take thou our suffrages, master, with gentleness.

---

[1] Du Méril, *op. cit.*, p. 239.

Paul, to our litanies lend an indulgent ear,
Who the philosophers vanquished with zeal severe :
Thou that art steward now in the Lord's heavenly
    house,
Give us to taste of the meat of grace bounteous ;
So that the wisdom which filled thee and nourished thee
May be our sustenance through the truths taught by thee."

A curious secular piece of the tenth century deserves
more than passing mention. It shows how wine,
women, and song, even in an age which is supposed to
have trembled for the coming destruction of the world,
still formed the attraction of some natures. What is
more, there is a certain modern, as distinguished from
classical, tone of tenderness in the sentiment. It is
the invitation of a young man to his mistress, bidding
her to a little supper in his rooms : [1] —

" Come therefore now, my gentle fere,
Whom as my heart I hold full dear ;
Enter my little room, which is
Adorned with quaintest rarities :
There are the seats with cushions spread,
The roof with curtains overhead ;
The house with flowers of sweetest scent
And scattered herbs is redolent :
A table there is deftly dight
With meats and drinks of rare delight ;

---

[1] Du Méril, *Poésies Populaires Latines du Moyen Age*, p. 196.

There too the wine flows, sparkling, free;
And all, my love, to pleasure thee.
There sound enchanting symphonies;
The clear high notes of flutes arise;
A singing girl and artful boy
Are chanting for thee strains of joy;
He touches with his quill the wire,
She tunes her note unto the lyre:
The servants carry to and fro
Dishes and cups of ruddy glow;
But these delights, I will confess,
Than pleasant converse charm me less;
Nor is the feast so sweet to me
As dear familiarity.
Then come now, sister of my heart,
That dearer than all others art,
Unto mine eyes thou shining sun,
Soul of my soul, thou only one!
I dwelt alone in the wild woods,
And loved all secret solitudes;
Oft would I fly from tumults far,
And shunned where crowds of people are.
O dearest, do not longer stay!
Seek we to live and love to-day!
I cannot live without thee, sweet!
Time bids us now our love complete.
Why should we then defer, my own,
What must be done or late or soon?
Do quickly what thou canst not shun!
I have no hesitation."

From Du Méril's collections further specimens of thoroughly secular poetry might be culled. Such is the panegyric of the nightingale, which contains the following impassioned lines : [1]—

> " Implet silvas atque cuncta modulis arbustula,
> Gloriosa valde facta veris prae laetitia ;
> Volitando scandit alta arborum cacumina,
> Ac festiva satis gliscit sibilare carmina."

Such are the sapphics on the spring, which, though they date from the seventh century, have a truly modern sentiment of Nature. Such, too, is the medieval legend of the Snow-Child, treated comically in burlesque Latin verse, and meant to be sung to a German tune of love—*Modus Liebinc*. To the same category may be referred the horrible, but singularly striking, series of Latin poems edited from a MS. at Berne, which set forth the miseries of monastic life with realistic passion bordering upon delirium, under titles like the following—*Dissuasio Concubitûs in Uno tantum Sexu*, or *De Monachi Cruciatu*.[2]

[1] Du Méril, *Poésies Pop. Lat. Ant.*, pp. 278, 241, 275.

[2] These extraordinary compositions will be found on pp. 174-182 of a closely-printed book entitled *Carmina Med. Aev. Max. Part. Inedita. Ed. H. Hagenus. Bernae. Ap. G. Frobenium.* MDCCCLXXVII. The editor, so far as I can discover, gives but scant indication of the poet who lurks,

VI

There is little need to dwell upon these crepuscular stirrings of popular Latin poetry in the earlier Middle Ages. To indicate their existence was necessary ; for they serve to link by a dim and fragile thread of evolution the decadent art of the base Empire with the renascence of paganism attempted in the twelfth century, and thus to connect that dawn of modern feeling with the orient splendours of the fourteenth and fifteenth centuries in Italy.

The first point to notice is the dominance of music in this verse, and the subjugation of the classic metres to its influence. A deeply significant transition has been effected from the *versus* to the *modulus* by the substitution of accent for quantity, and by the value given to purely melodic cadences. A long syllable and a short syllable have almost equal weight in this prosody, for the musical tone can be prolonged or shortened upon either. So now the *cantilena*, rather than the *metron*, rules the flow of verse ; but, at the same time, antique

---

with so much style and so terrible emotions, under the veil of Cod. Bern., 702 s. Any student who desires to cut into the core of cloister life should read cvii. pp. 178–182, of this little book.

forms are still conventionally used, though violated in
the using.   In other words, the modern metres of the
modern European races—the Italian Hendecasyllable,
the French Alexandrine, the English Iambic and
Trochaic rhythms—have been indicated ; and a moment
has been prepared when these measures shall tune themselves by means of emphasis and accent to song, before
they take their place as literary schemes appealing to
the ear in rhetoric.   This phase, whereby the metres of
antiquity pass into the rhythms of the modern races,
implies the use of medieval Latin, still not unmindful
of classic art, but governed now by music often of
Teutonic origin, and further modified by affinities of
prosody imported from Teutonic sources.

The next point to note is that, in this process of
transition, popular ecclesiastical poetry takes pre-
cedence of secular.   The great rhyming structures of
the Middle Ages, which exercised so wide an influence
over early European literature, were invented for the
service of the Church—voluminous systems of recurrent
double rhymes, intricate rhythms moulded upon tunes
for chanting, solid melodic fabrics, which, having once
been formed, were used for lighter efforts of the fancy,
or lent their ponderous effects to parody.   Thus, in the
first half of the centuries which intervene between the

extinction of the genuine Roman Empire and the year
1300, ecclesiastical poetry took the lead in creating
and popularising new established types of verse, and in
rendering the spoken Latin pliable for various purposes
of art.

A third point worthy of attention is, that a certain
breath of paganism, wafting perfumes from the old
mythology, whispering of gods in exile, encouraging
men to accept their life on earth with genial enjoyment,
was never wholly absent during the darkest periods of
the Middle Ages.   This inspiration uttered itself in
Latin ; for we have little reason to believe that the
modern languages had yet attained plasticity enough for
the expression of that specific note which belongs to
the Renaissance—the note of humanity conscious of
its Græco-Roman pagan past.   This Latin, meanwhile, which it employed was fabricated by the Church
and used by men of learning.

VII

The songs of the Wandering Students were in a strict
sense *moduli* as distinguished from *versus ;* popular and
not scholastic.   They were, however, composed by

men of culture, imbued with classical learning of some
sort, and prepared by scholarship for the deftest and
most delicate manipulation of the Latin language.

Who were these Wandering Students, so often mentioned, and of whom nothing has been as yet related?
As their name implies, they were men, and for the most
part young men, travelling from university to university
in search of knowledge.   Far from their homes, without responsibilities, light of purse and light of heart,
careless and pleasure-seeking, they ran a free, disreput-
able course, frequenting taverns at least as much as
lecture-rooms, more capable of pronouncing judgment upon wine or women than upon a problem of
divinity or logic.   The conditions of medieval learning
made it necessary to study different sciences in different
parts of Europe; and a fixed habit of unrest, which
seems to have pervaded society after the period of the
Crusades, encouraged vagabondage in all classes.   The
extent to which travelling was carried in the Middle
Ages for purposes of pilgrimage and commerce, out of
pure curiosity or love of knowledge, for the bettering
of trade in handicrafts or for self-improvement in the
sciences, has only of late years been estimated at a just
calculation.   "The scholars," wrote a monk of Froid-
mont in the twelfth century, "are wont to roam around

the world and visit all its cities, till much learning makes them mad; for in Paris they seek liberal arts, in Orleans authors, at Salerno gallipots, at Toledo demons, and in no place decent manners."

These pilgrims to the shrines of knowledge formed a class apart. They were distinguished from the secular and religious clergy, inasmuch as they had taken no orders, or only minor orders, held no benefice or cure, and had entered into no conventual community. They were still more sharply distinguished from the laity, whom they scorned as brutes, and with whom they seem to have lived on terms of mutual hostility. One of these vagabond gownsmen would scarcely condescend to drink with a townsman:[1]—

> "In aeterno igni
> Cruciantur rustici, qui non sunt tam digni
> Quod bibisse noverint bonum vinum vini."

> "Aestimetur laicus ut brutus,
> Nam ad artem surdus est et mutus."

> "Litteratos convocat decus virginale,
> Laicorum execrat pectus bestiale."

---

[1] See the drinking song printed in *Walter Mapes*, p. xlv., and *Carm. Bur.*, pp. 198, 179.

In a parody of the Mass, which is called *Officium Lusorum,* and in which the prayers are offered to Bacchus, we find this devout collect : [1]—" Omnipotens sempiterne deus, qui inter rusticos et clericos magnam discordiam seminasti, praesta quaesumus de laboribus eorum vivere, de mulieribus ipsorum vero et de morte deciorum semper gaudere."

The English version of this ribald prayer is even more explicit. It runs thus :—" Deus qui multitudinem rusticorum ad servitium clericorum venire fecisti et militum et inter nos et ipsos discordiam seminasti."

It is open to doubt whether the *milites* or soldiers were included with the rustics in that laity, for which the students felt so bitter a contempt. But the tenor of some poems on love, especially the *Dispute of Phyllis and Flora,* shows that the student claimed a certain superiority over the soldier. This antagonism between clerk and rustic was heartily reciprocated. In a song on taverns the student is warned that he may meet with rough treatment from the clodhopper : [2]—

1 *Carm. Bur.*, p. 249, note. There is a variation in the parody printed by Wright, *Rel. Antiq.*, ii.

2 See A. P. von Bärnstein's little volume, *Ubi sunt qui ante nos*, p. 46.

> "O clerici dilecti,
>   Discite vitare
> Tabernam horribilem,
>   Qui cupitis regnare;
> Nec audeant vos rustici
>   Plagis verberare!
>
> Rusticus dum se
>   Sentit ebriatum,
> Clericum non reputat
>   Militem armatum.
> Vere plane consulo
>   Ut abstineatis,
> Nec unquam cum rusticis
>   Tabernam ineatis."

The affinities of the Wandering Students were rather with the Church than with laymen of any degree. They piqued themselves upon their title of *Clerici*, and added the epithet of *Vagi*. We shall see in the sequel that they stood in a peculiar relation of dependence upon ecclesiastical society.

According to tendencies prevalent in the Middle Ages, they became a sort of guild, and proclaimed themselves with pride an Order. Nothing is more clearly marked in their poetry than the *esprit de corps*, which animates them with a cordial sense of brotherhood.[1]

[1] See especially the songs *Ordo Noster* and *Nos Vagabunduli*, translated below in Section xiii.

The same tendencies which prompted their association required that they should have a patron saint. But as the confraternity was anything but religious, this saint, or rather this eponymous hero, had to be a Rabelaisian character. He was called Golias, and his flock received the generic name of Goliardi. Golias was father and master; the Goliardi were his family, his sons, and pupils. *Familia Goliae, Magister Golias, Pueri Goliae, Discipulus Goliae*, are phrases to be culled from the rubrics of their literature.

Much has been conjectured regarding these names and titles. Was Golias a real person? Did he give his own name to the Goliardi; or was he invented after the Goliardi had already acquired their designation? In either case, ought we to connect both words with the Latin *gula*, and so regard the Goliardi as notable gluttons; or with the Provençal *goliar, gualiar, gualiardor*, which carry a significance of deceit? Had Golias anything to do with Goliath of the Bible, the great Philistine, who in the present day would more properly be chosen as the hero of those classes which the students held in horror?

It is not easy to answer these questions. All we know for certain is, that the term Goliardus was in common medieval use, and was employed as a synonym for Wandering Scholar in ecclesiastical documents. *Vagi scholares aut Goliardi—joculatores, goliardi seu bufones—goliardia vel histrionatus—vagi scholares qui goliardi vel histriones alio nomine appellantur—clerici ribaudi, maxime qui dicuntur de familia Goliae :* so run the acts of several Church Councils.[1] The word passed into modern languages. The *Grandes Chroniques de S. Denis* speak of *jugleor, enchanteor, goliardois, et autres manières de menestrieux.* Chaucer, in his description of the Miller, calls this merry narrator of fabliaux *a jangler and a goliardeis.* In *Piers Ploughman* the *goliardeis* is further explained to be *a glutton of words,* and talks in Latin rhyme.[2]

Giraldus Cambrensis, during whose lifetime the name Golias first came into vogue, thought that this father of the Goliardic family was a real person.[3] He writes of him thus :—"A certain parasite called **Golias,** who in our time obtained wide notoriety for his gluttony and lechery, and by addiction to gulosity and debauchery deserved his surname, being of excellent culture but of bad manners, and of no moral discipline, uttered oftentimes and in many forms, both of rhythm and metre, infamous libels against the Pope and Curia of Rome,

[1] See Wright's introduction to *Walter Mapes.*
[2] Ibid.
[3] Ibid.

with no less impudence than imprudence." This is perhaps the most outspoken utterance with regard to the eponymous hero of the Goliardic class which we possess, and it deserves a close inspection.

In the first place, Giraldus attributes the satiric poems which passed under the name of Golias to a single author famous in his days, and says of this poet that he used both modern rhythms and classical metres. The description would apply to Gualtherus de Insula, Walter of Lille, or, as he is also called, Walter of Chatillon; for some of this Walter's satires are composed in a curious mixture of the rhyming measures of the medieval hymns with classical hexameters.[1] Yet had Giraldus been pointing at Walter of Lille, a notable personage in his times, there is no good reason to suppose that he would have suppressed his real name, or have taken for granted that Golias was a *bona fide* surname. On the theory that he knew Golias to be a mere nickname, and was aware that Walter of Lille was the actual satirist, we should have to explain his paragraph by the hypothesis that he chose to sneer at

[1] See Müldner, *Die zehn Gedichte des Walther von Lille*, 1859. Walter Mapes (ed. Wright) is credited with five of these satires, including two which close each stanza with a hexameter from Juvenal, Virgil, Ovid, Lucan, Horace.

him under his *nom de guerre* instead of stigmatising him openly in person.

His remarks, at any rate, go far toward disposing of the old belief that the Goliardic satires were the work of Thomas Mapes. Giraldus was an intimate friend of that worthy, who deserves well of all lovers of medieval romance as a principal contributor to the Arthurian cycle. It is hardly possible that Giraldus should have gibbeted such a man under the sobriquet of Golias.

But what, it may be asked, if Walter of Lille, without the cognisance of our English annalist, had in France obtained the chief fame of these poems? what if they afterwards were attributed in England to another Walter, his contemporary, himself a satirist of the monastic orders? The fact that Walter of Lille was known in Latin as Gualtherus de Insula, or Walter of the Island, may have confirmed the misapprehension thus suggested. It should be added that the ascription of the Goliardic satires to Walter Mapes or Map first occurs in MSS. of the fourteenth century.

VIII

I do not think there is much probability of arriving at certainty with regard to the problems indicated in the foregoing section. We must be content to accept the names Golias and Goliardi as we find them, and to treat of this literature as the product of a class, from the midst of which, as it is clear to any critic, more than one poet rose to eminence.

One thing appears manifest from the references to the Goliardi which I have already quoted. That is, that the Wandering Students ranked in common estimation with jongleurs, buffoons, and minstrels. Both classes held a similar place in medieval society. Both were parasites devoted to the entertainment of their superiors in rank. Both were unattached, except by occasional engagements, to any fixed abode. But while the minstrels found their temporary homes in the castles of the nobility, we have reason to believe that the Goliardi haunted abbeys and amused the leisure of ecclesiastical lords.

The personality of the writer disappears in nearly all the *Carmina Vagorum*. Instead of a poet with a name, we find a type; and the verse is put into the mouth of

Golias himself, or the Archipoeta, or the Primate of the order. This merging of the individual in the class of which he forms a part is eminently characteristic of popular literature, and separates the Goliardic songs from those of the Provençal Troubadours. The emotions to which popular poetry gives expression are generic rather than personal. They are such that all the world, granted common sympathies and common proclivities, can feel them and adopt the mode of utterance invented for them by the singer. If there be any bar to their universal acceptance, it is only such as may belong to the peculiar conditions of the social class from which they have emanated. The *Rispetti* of Tuscany imply a certain form of peasant life. The *Carmina Vagorum* are coloured to some extent by the prejudices and proclivities of vagabond existence.

Trenchantly true as the inspiration of a popular lyric may be, inevitable as may be the justice of its sentiment, unerring as may be its touch upon reality, still it lacks the note which marks it out for one man's utterance among a thousand. Composing it, the one has made himself the mouthpiece of the thousand. What the *Volkslied* gains in universality it loses in individuality of character. Its applicability to human nature at large is obtained at the sacrifice of that

interest which belongs to special circumstances. It
suits every one who grieves or loves or triumphs. It
does not indicate the love, the grief, the triumph of
this man and no other. It possesses the pathos and
the beauty of countless human lives prolonged through
inarticulate generations, finding utterance at last in it.
It is deficient in that particular intonation which makes
a Shelley's voice differ from a Leopardi's, Petrarch's
sonnets for Laura differ from Sidney's sonnets for
Stella. It has always less of perceptible artistic effect,
more enduring human quality. Some few of its lines
are so well found, so rightly said, that they possess the
certainty of natural things—a quality rare in the works
of all but the greatest known poets. But these phrases
with the accent of truest truth are often embedded in
mere generalities and repetitions.

These characteristics of popular poetry help to
explain the frequent recurrence of the same ideas, the
same expressions, the same stanzas even, in the lyrics
of the Goliardi. A *Volkslied*, once created, becomes
common property. It flies abroad like thistledown;
settles and sows its seed; is maimed and mutilated;
is improved or altered for the worse; is curtailed,
expanded, adapted to divers purposes at different times
and in very different relations.

We may dismiss the problem of authorship partly as insoluble, partly as of slight importance for a literature which is manifestly popular. With even greater brevity may the problem of nationality be disposed of. Some critics have claimed an Italian, some an English, some a French, and some a German origin for the *Carmina Vagorum.* The truth is that, just as the *Clerici Vagi* were themselves of all nations, so were their songs; and the use of a Latin common to all Europe in the Middle Ages renders it difficult even to conjecture the soil from which any particular lyric may have sprung. As is natural, a German codex contains more songs of Teutonic origin; an English displays greater abundance of English compositions. I have already observed that our two chief sources of Goliardic literature have many elements in common; but the treasures of the Benedictbeuern MS. differ in complexion from those of the Harleian in important minor details; and it is probable that if French and Italian stores were properly ransacked—which has not yet been done—we should note in them similar characteristic divergences.

The *Carmina Burana*, by their frequent references to linden-trees and nightingales, and their numerous German refrains, indicate a German home for the poems on

spring and love, in which they are specially rich.[1]
The collections of our own land have an English turn
of political thought; the names Anglia and Anglus not
unfrequently occur; and the use of the word " Schel-
linck " in one of the *Carmina Burana* may point, perhaps, to an English origin.   France claims her own,
not only in the acknowledged pieces of Walter de
Lille, but also in a few which exhibit old French
refrains.   To Italian conditions, if not to Italian poets,
we may refer those that introduce spreading pines or
olive-trees into their pictures, and one which yields the
refrain *Bela mia*.   The most important lyric of the
series, *Golias' Confession*, was undoubtedly written at
Pavia, but whether by an Italian or not we do not
know.   The probability is rather, perhaps, in favour of
Teutonic authorship, since this *Confession* is addressed
to a German prelate.   Here it may be noticed that
the proper names of places and people are frequently
altered to suit different countries ; while in some cases
they are indicated by an N, sufficiently suggestive of
their generality.   Thus the *Confession of Golias* in the

---

[1] The more I study the songs of love and wine in this
codex, the more convinced am I that they have their origin
for the most part in South-Western Germany, Bavaria, the
Bodensee, and Elsass.

Carmina Burana mentions *Electe Coloniae ;* in an English version, introduces *Praesul Coventriae.* The prayer for alms, which I have translated in Section xiii., is addressed to *Decus N——,* thou honour of Norwich town, or Wittenberg, or wherever the wandering scholar may have chanced to be.

With regard to the form and diction of the *Carmina Vagorum,* it is enough to say two things at the present time. First, a large portion of these pieces, including a majority of the satires and longer descriptive poems, are composed in measures borrowed from hymnology, follow the diction of the Church, and imitate the double-rhyming rhythms of her sequences. It is not unnatural, this being the case, that parodies of hymns should be comparatively common. Of these I shall produce some specimens in the course of this study. Secondly, those which do not exhibit popular hymn measures are clearly written for melodies, some of them very complicated in structure, suggesting part-songs and madrigals, with curious interlacing of long and short lines, double and single rhymes, recurrent ritournelles, and so forth.

The ingenuity with which these poets adapted their language to the exigencies of the tune, taxing the fertility of Latin rhymes, and setting off the long

sonorous words to great advantage, deserves admiring
comment.   At their best, it is almost impossible to
reproduce in English the peculiar effects of their
melodic artifices.   But there is another side to the
matter.   At their worst, these Latin lyrics, moulded
on a tune, degenerate into disjointed verbiage, sound
and adaptation to song prevailing over sense and satisfaction to the mind.   It must, however, be remembered
that such lyrics, sometimes now almost unintelligible,
have come down to us with a very mutilated text, after
suffering the degradations through frequent oral trans-
mission to which popular poetry is peculiarly liable.

IX

It is easier to say what the Goliardi wrote about
than who the writers were, and what they felt and
thought than by what names they were baptised.   The
mass of their literature, as it is at present known to us,
divides into two broad classes.   The one division in-
cludes poems on the themes of vagabond existence, the
truant life of these capricious students; on springtime
and its rural pleasure; on love in many phases and for
divers kinds of women; lastly, on wine and on the

dice-box. The other division is devoted to graver topics; to satires on society, touching especially the Roman Court, and criticising eminent ecclesiastics in all countries; to moral dissertations, and to discourses on the brevity of life.

Of the two divisions, the former yields by far the livelier image of the men we have to deal with. It will therefore form the staple of my argument. The latter blends at so many points with medieval literature of the monastic kind, that it is chiefly distinguished by boldness of censure and sincerity of invective. In these qualities the serious poems of the Goliardi, emanating from a class of men who moved behind the scenes and yet were free to speak their thoughts, are unique. Written with the satirist's eye upon the object of his sarcasm, tinged with the license of his vagabondage, throbbing with the passionate and nonchalant afflatus of the wine-cup, they wing their flight like poisoned arrows or plumed serpents with unerring straightness at abuses in high places.

The wide space occupied by Nature in the secular poems of the Goliardi is remarkable. As a background to their love-songs we always find the woods and fields of May, abundant flowers and gushing rivulets, lime-trees and pines and olive-trees, through which soft

winds are blowing. There are rose-bowers and nightin
gales; fauns, nymphs, and satyrs dancing on the sward.
Choirs of mortal maidens emerge in the midst of this
Claude-landscape. The scene, meanwhile, has been
painted from experience, and felt with the enthusiasm
of affection. It breathes of healthy open air, of life
upon the road, of casual joys and wayside pleasure,
snatched with careless heart by men whose tastes are
natural. There is very little of the alcove or the
closet in this verse; and the touch upon the world is
so infantine, so tender, that we are indulgent to the
generalities with which the poets deal.

What has been said about popular poetry applies
also to popular painting. In the landscapes of Goliardic
literature there is nothing specific to a single locality—
no name like Vaucluse, no pregnant touch that indicates
one scene selected from a thousand. The landscape is
always a background, more northern or more southern
as the case may be, but penetrated with the feeling of
the man who has been happy or has suffered there.
This feeling, broadly, sensuously diffused, as in a
masterpiece of Titian, prepares us for the human
element to be exhibited.

The foreground of these pictures is occupied by a
pair of lovers meeting after the long winter's separation,

a dance upon the village green, a young man gazing on the mistress he adores, a disconsolate exile from his home, the courtship of a student and a rustic beauty, or perhaps the grieved and melancholy figure of one whose sweetheart has proved faithless. Such actors in the comedy of life are defined with fervent intensity of touch against the leafy vistas of the scene. The lyrical cry emerges clear and sharp in all that concerns their humanity.

The quality of love expressed is far from being either platonic or chivalrous. It is love of the sensuous, impulsive, appetitive kind, to which we give the name of Pagan. The finest outbursts of passion are emanations from a potent sexual desire. Meanwhile, nothing indicates the character or moral quality of either man or woman. The student and the girl are always *vis-à-vis*, fixed characters in this lyrical love-drama. He calls her Phyllis, Flora, Lydia, Glycerion, Caecilia. He remains unnamed, his physical emotion sufficing for personal description. The divinity presiding over them is Venus. Jove and Danae, Cupid and the Graces, Paris and Helen, follow in her train. All the current classical mythology is laid under cheap contribution. Yet the central emotion, the young man's heart's desire, is so vividly portrayed, that we seem to be overhearing the triumphant ebullition or the melancholy love-lament of a real soul.

X

The sentiment of love is so important in the songs of the Wandering Students, that it may not be superfluous at this point to cull a few emphatic phrases which illustrate the core of their emotion, and to present these in the original Latin.

I may first observe to what a large extent the ideas of spring and of female society were connected at that epoch. Winter was a dreary period, during which a man bore his fate and suffered. He emerged from it into sunshine, brightened by the intercourse with women, which was then made possible. This is how the winter is described : [1] —

> "In omni loco congruo
> Sermonis oblectatio
> Cum sexu femineo
> Evanuit omni modo."

Of the true love-songs, only one refers expressly to the winter season. That, however, is the lyric upon

[1] *Carm. Bur.*, p. 174.

Flora, which contains a detailed study of plastic form
in the bold spirit of the Goliardic style.[1]

The particularity with which the personal charms of
women are described deserves attention.   The portrait
of Flora, to which I have just alluded, might be cited
as one of the best specimens.   But the slightest shades
are discriminated, as in this touch :[2] —

> " Labellulis
> Castigate tumentibus."

One girl has long tawny tresses : *Caesaries subrubea*.
Another is praised for the masses of her dark hair :
Frons nimirum coronata, supercilium nigrata.   Roses
and lilies vie, of course, upon the cheeks of all ; and
sometimes their sweetness surpasses the lily of the
valley.   From time to time a touch of truer poetry
occurs ; as, for instance [3]—

> " O decora super ora
> Belli Absalonis ! "

Or take again the outburst of passion in this stanza,
where both the rhythm and the ponderous Latin
words, together with the abrupt transition from the
third to the fourth line, express a fine exaltation : [4]—

[1] *Carm. Bur.*, p. 149, translated below in Section xvii.
[2] Ibid., p. 130.   [3] Ibid., p. 200.
          [4] Ibid., p. 231.

> " Frons et gula, labra, mentum
>   Dant amoris alimentum;
>   Crines ejus adamavi,
>   Quoniam fuere flavi."

The same kind of enthusiasm is more elaborately worked out in the following comparisons : [1]—

> " Matutini sideris
>   Jubar praeis,
>   Et lilium
>   Rosaque periere:
>   Micat ebur dentium
>   Per labium,
>   Ut Sirium
>   Credat quis enitere."

As might be expected, such lovers were not satisfied with contemplative pleasures : [2]—

> " Visu, colloquio,
>   Contactu, basio,
>   Frui virgo dederat;
>   Sed aberat
>   Linea posterior
>   Et melior amori,
>   Quam nisi transiero,
>   De cetero
>   Sunt quae dantur alia
>   Materia furori,"

---

[1] *Carm. Bur.*, p. 121.   [2] Ibid., p. 135.

The conclusion of this song, which, taken in its integrity, deserves to be regarded as typical of what is pagan in this erotic literature, may be studied in the Appendix to *Carmina Burana*.

Occasionally the lover's desire touches a higher point of spirituality : [1]—

> " Non tactu sanabor labiorum,
>   Nisi cor unum fiat duorum
>   Et idem velle.   Vale, flos florum ! "

Occasionally, the sensuous fervour assumes a passionate intensity : [2]—

> " Nocte cum ea si dormiero,
>   Si sua labra semel suxero,
>   Mortem subire, placenter obire, vitamque finire,
>   Libens potero."

Very rarely there is a strong desire expressed for fidelity, as in a beautiful lyric of absence, which I hope to give translated in full in my 17th Section.

But the end to be attained is always such as is summed up in these brief words placed upon a girl's lips : [3]—

Carm. Bur , p. 145.   [2] Ibid., p. 230
[3] Ibid., p. 133.

> " Dulcissime,
> Totam tibi subdo me."

And the motto of both sexes is this : [1]—

> " Quicquid agant alii,
> Juvenes amemus."

It may be added, in conclusion, that the sweethearts of our students seem to have been mostly girls of the working and rustic classes, sometimes women of bad fame, rarely married women.   In no case that has come beneath my notice is there any hint that one of them aspired to such amours with noble ladies as distinguished the Troubadours.   A democratic tone, a tone of the proletariate, is rather strangely blent with the display of learning, and with the more than common literary skill apparent in their work.

XI

The drinking-songs are equally spontaneous and fresh.   Anacreon pales before the brilliancy of the Archipoeta when wine is in his veins, and the fountain of the Bacchic chant swells with gushes of strongly

[1] *Carm. Bur.*, p. 251.

emphasised bold double rhymes, each throbbing like a man's firm stroke upon the strings of lyres. A fine audacity breathes through the praises of the wine-god, sometimes rising to lyric rapture, sometimes sinking to parody and innuendo, but always carrying the bard on rolling wheels along the paths of song. The reality of the inspiration is indubitable. These Bacchanalian choruses have been indited in the tavern, with a crowd of topers round the poet, with the rattle of the dice-box ringing in his ears, and with the facile maidens of his volatile amours draining the wine-cup at his elbow.

Wine is celebrated as the source of pleasure in social life, provocative of love, parent of poetry : [1]—

> "Bacchus forte superans
> Pectora virorum
> In amorem concitat
> Animos eorum.
>
> Bacchus saepe visitans
> Mulierum genus
> Facit eas subditas
> Tibi, O tu Venus ! "

From his temple, the tavern, water-drinkers and fastidious persons are peremptorily warned : [2]—

[1] *Carm. Bur.*, p. 238.   [2] Ibid., p. 240.

> " Qui potare not potestis,
>   Ite procul ab his festis ;
>   Non est hic locus modestis :
>   Devitantur plus quam pestis."

The tavern is loved better than the church, and a
bowl of wine than the sacramental chalice : [1]—

> " Magis quam ecclesiam
>   Diligo tabernam."

> " Mihi sapit dulcius
>   Vinum de taberna,
>   Quam quod aqua miscuit
>   Praesulis pincerna."

As in the love-songs, so in these drinking-songs we
find no lack of mythological allusions. Nor are the
grammatical quibbles, which might also have been
indicated as a defect of the erotic poetry, conspicuous
by absence. But both alike are impotent to break
the spell of evident sincerity. We discount them as
belonging to the euphuism of a certain epoch, and are
rather surprised than otherwise that they should not be
more apparent. The real and serious defect of Goliardic literature is not affectation, but something very
different, which I shall try to indicate in the last
Section of this treatise. Venus and Helen, Liber and

[1] Wright's *Walter Mapes*, p. xlv. ; *Carm. Bur.*, p. 69.

Lyaeus, are but the current coin of poetic diction common to the whole student class. These Olympian deities merge without a note of discord into the dim background of a medieval pothouse or the sylvan shades of some ephemeral amour, leaving the realism of natural appetite in either case untouched.

It is by no means the thin and conventional sprinkling of classical erudition which makes these poems of the Goliardi pagan, and reminds the student of Renaissance art. Conversely, the scholastic plays on words which they contain do not stamp them out as medieval. Both of these qualities are *rococo* and superficial rather than essential and distinctive in their style. After making due allowances for either element of oddity, a true connoisseur will gratefully appreciate the spontaneous note of enjoyment, the disengagement from ties and duties imposed by temporal respectability, the frank animalism, which connects these vivid hymns to Bacchus and Venus with past Aristophanes and future Rabelais. They celebrate the eternal presence of mirth-making powers in hearts of men, apart from time and place and varying dogmas which do not concern deities of Nature.

XII

The time has now come for me to introduce my reader to the versions I have made from the songs of Wandering Students. I must remind him that, while the majority of these translations aim at literal exactness and close imitation of the originals in rhyme and structure, others are more paraphrastic. It has always been my creed that a good translation should resemble a plaster-cast; the English being *plaqué* upon the original, so as to reproduce its exact form, although it cannot convey the effects of bronze or marble, which belong to the material of the work of art. But this method has not always seemed to me the most desirable for rendering poems, an eminent quality of which is facility and spontaneity. In order to obtain that quality in our language, the form has occasionally to be sacrificed.

What Coleridge has reported to have said of Southey may be applied to a translator. He too " is in some sort like an elegant setter of jewels ; the stones are not his own: he gives them all the advantage of his art, but not their native brilliancy." I feel even more than this when I attempt translation, and reflect

that, unlike the jeweller, it is my doom to reduce the
lustre of the gems I handle, even if I do not substitute
paste and pebbles. Yet I am frequently enticed to
repeat experiments, which afterwards I regard in the
light of failures. What allures me first is the pleasure
of passing into that intimate familiarity with art which
only a copyist or a translator enjoys. I am next im-
pelled by the desire to fix the attention of readers on
things which I admire, and which are possibly beyond
their scope of view. Lastly comes that *ignis fatuus* of
the hope, for ever renewed, if also for ever disappointed,
that some addition may be made in this way to the
wealth of English poetry. A few exquisite pieces in
Latin literature, the Catullian *Ille mi par*, for example,
a few in our own, such as Jonson's *Drink to me only
with thine eyes*, are translations. Possibly the miracle
of such poetic transmutation may be repeated for me ;
possibly an English song may come to birth by my
means also. With this hope in view, the translator is
strongly tempted to engraft upon his versions elegances
in the spirit of his native language, or to use the
motives of the original for improvisations in his own
manner. I must plead guilty to having here and there
yielded to this temptation, as may appear upon comparison of my English with the Latin. All translation

is a compromise; and while being conscious of having to sacrifice much, the translator finds himself often seeking to add something as a makeweight.

I shall divide my specimens into nine Sections. The first will include those which deal with the Order of Wandering Students in general, winding up with the *Confession* ascribed to Golias, the father of the family. The second, third, fourth, and fifth are closely connected, since they contain spring-songs, pastorals, descriptive poems touching upon love, and erotic lyrics. The sixth Section will be devoted to a few songs of exile, doubt, and sorrow. In the seventh we shall reach anacreontics on the theme of wine, passing in the eighth to parodies and comic pieces. Four or five serious compositions will close the list in the ninth Section.

At the end of the book I mean to print a table containing detailed references to the originals of the songs I have chosen for translation, together with an index of the principal works that have been published on this subject.

XIII

The first song which concerns the Order of
Wandering Students in general has been attributed to
the Archipoeta or head-bard of the guild.   Whoever
this poet may have been, it is to him that we owe the
Confession of Golias, by far the most spirited composition of the whole Goliardic species.   I do not
think the style of the poem on the Order, though it
belongs to a good period, justifies our ascribing it to so
inspired and genial a lyrist.

The argument runs as follows.   Just as commission
was given to the Apostles to go forth and preach in
the whole world, so have the Wandering Students a
vocation to travel, and to test the hearts of men wherever they may sojourn.   A burlesque turn is given to
this function of the *Vagi*.   Yet their consciousness of
a satiric mission, their willingness to pose as critics of
society from the independent vantage-ground of vagabondage, seems seriously hinted at.

The chief part of the song is devoted to a description of the comprehensive nature of the Order, which
receives all sorts and conditions of men, and makes no
distinction of nationality.   The habitual poverty of its

THE ORDER OF WANDERING
STUDENTS

No. 1

A T the mandate, Go ye forth,
    Through the whole world hurry!
Priests tramp out toward south and north,
    Monks and hermits skurry,
Levites smooth the gospel leave,
    Bent on ambulation;
Each and all to our sect cleave,
    Which is life's salvation.

In this sect of ours 'tis writ:
    Prove all things in season;
Weigh this life and judge of it
    By your riper reason;
'Gainst all evil clerks be you
    Steadfast in resistance,
Who refuse large tithe and due
    Unto your subsistence.

Marquesses, Bavarians,
　　Austrians and Saxons,
Noblemen and chiefs of clans,
　　Glorious by your actions !
Listen, comrades all, I pray,
　　To these new decretals :
Misers they must meet decay,
　　Niggardly gold-beetles.

We the laws of charity
　　Found, nor let them crumble ;
For into our order we
　　Take both high and humble :
Rich and poor men we receive,
　　In our bosom cherish ;
Welcome those the shavelings leave
　　At their doors to perish.

We receive the tonsured monk,
　　Let him take his pittance ;
And the parson with his punk,
　　If he craves admittance ;
Masters with their bands of boys,
　　Priests with high dominion ;
But the scholar who enjoys
　　Just one coat's our minion !

This our sect doth entertain
   Just men and unjust ones ;
Halt, lame, weak of limb or brain,
   Strong men and robust ones ;
Those who flourish in their pride,
   Those whom age makes stupid ;
Frigid folk and hot folk fried
   In the fires of Cupid.

Tranquil souls and bellicose,
   Peacemaker and foeman ;
Czech and Hun, and mixed with those
   German, Slav, and Roman ;
Men of middling size and weight,
   Dwarfs and giants mighty ;
Men of modest heart and state,
   Vain men, proud and flighty.

Of the Wanderers' order I
   Tell the Legislature—
They whose life is free and high,
   Gentle too their nature—
They who'd rather scrape a fat
   Dish in gravy swimming,
Than in sooth to marvel at
   Barns with barley brimming.

Now this order, as I ken,
  Is called sect or section,
Since its sectaries are men
  Divers in complexion ;
Therefore *hic* and *haec* and *hoc*
  Suit it in declension,
Since so multiform a flock
  Here finds comprehension.

This our order hath decried
  Matins with a warning ;
For that certain phantoms glide
  In the early morning,
Whereby pass into man's brain
  Visions of vain folly ;
Early risers are insane,
  Racked by melancholy.

This our order doth proscribe
  All the year round matins ;
When they've left their beds, our tribe
  In the tap sing latins ;
There they call for wine for all,
  Roasted fowl and chicken ;
Hazard's threats no hearts appal,
  Though his strokes still thicken.

This our order doth forbid
　　Double clothes with loathing :
He whose nakedness is hid
　　With one vest hath clothing :
Soon one throws his cloak aside
　　At the dice-box' calling ;
Next his girdle is untied,
　　While the cards are falling.

What I've said of upper clothes
　　To the nether reaches ;
They who own a shirt, let those
　　Think no more of breeches ;
If one boasts big boots to use,
　　Let him leave his gaiters ;
They who this firm law refuse
　　Shall be counted traitors.

No one, none shall wander forth
　　Fasting from the table ;
If thou'rt poor, from south and north
　　Beg as thou art able
Hath it not been often seen
　　That one coin brings many,
When a gamester on the green
　　Stakes his lucky penny ?

No one on the road should walk
  'Gainst the wind—'tis madness ;
Nor in poverty shall stalk
  With a face of sadness ;
Let him bear him bravely then,
  Hope sustain his spirit ;
After heavy trials men
  Better luck inherit !

While throughout the world you rove,
  Thus uphold your banners ;
Give these reasons why you prove
  Hearts of men and manners :
" To reprove the reprobate,
  Probity approving,
Improbate from approbate
  To remove, I'm moving."

The next song is a lament for the decay of the
Order and the suppression of its privileges. It was
written, to all appearances, at a later date, and is
inferior in style. The Goliardi had already, we
learn from it, exchanged poverty for luxury. Instead
of tramping on the hard hoof, they moved with a
retinue of mounted servants. We seem to trace in the

lament a change from habits of simple vagabondage to
professional dependence, as minstrels and secretaries,
upon men of rank in Church and State, which came
over the Goliardic class. This poem, it may be
mentioned, does not occur in the *Carmina Burana*, nor
is it included among those which bear the name
of Walter Mapes or Map.

ON THE DECAY OF THE ORDER

No. 2

ONCE (it was in days of yore)
  This our order flourished;
Popes, whom Cardinals adore,
  It with honours nourished;
Licences desirable
  They gave, nought desiring;
While our prayers, the beads we tell,
  Served us for our hiring.

Now this order (so time runs)
  Is made tributary;
With the ruck of Adam's sons
  We must draw and carry;

Ground by common serfdom down,
    By our debts confounded,
Debts to market-place and town
    With the Jews compounded.

Once ('twas when the simple state
    Of our order lasted)
All men praised us, no man's hate
    Harried us or wasted ;
Rates and taxes on our crew
    There was none to levy ;
But the sect, douce men and true,
    Served God in a bevy.

Now some envious folks, who spy
    Sumptuous equipages,
Horses, litters passing by,
    And a host of pages,
Say, "Unless their purses were
    Quite with wealth o'erflowing,
They could never thus, I swear,
    Round about be going ! "

Such men do not think nor own
    How with toil we bend us,
Not to feed ourselves alone,
    But the folk who tend us :

On all comers, all who come,
    We our substance lavish,
Therefore 'tis a trifling sum
    For ourselves we ravish.

On this subject, at this time,
    What we've said suffices:
Let us leave it, lead the rhyme
    Back to our devices:
We the miseries of this life
    Bear with cheerful spirit,
That Heaven's bounty after strife
    We may duly merit.

'Tis a sign that God the Lord
    Will not let us perish,
Since with scourge and rod and sword
    He our souls doth cherish;
He amid this vale of woes
    Makes us bear the burden,
That true joys in heaven's repose
    May be ours for guerdon.

Next in order to these poems, which display the
Wandering Students as a class, I will produce two

that exhibit their mode of life in detail. The first is a begging petition, addressed by a scholar on the tramp to the great man of the place where he is staying. The name of the place, as I have already noticed, is only indicated by an N. The nasal whine of a suppliant for alms, begging, as Erasmus begged, not in the name of charity, but of learning, makes itself heard both in the rhyme and rhythm of the original Latin. I have tried to follow the sing-song doggerel.

A WANDERING STUDENT'S PETITION

No. 3

I, A wandering scholar lad,
    Born for toil and sadness,
Oftentimes am driven by
    Poverty to madness.

Literature and knowledge I
    Fain would still be earning,
Were it not that want of pelf
    Makes me cease from learning.

These torn clothes that cover me
   Are too thin and rotten;
Oft I have to suffer cold,
   By the warmth forgotten.

Scarce I can attend at church,
   Sing God's praises duly;
Mass and vespers both I miss,
   Though I love them truly.

Oh, thou pride of N——,
   By thy worth I pray thee
Give the suppliant help in need,
   Heaven will sure repay thee.

Take a mind unto thee now
   Like unto St. Martin;
Clothe the pilgrim's nakedness,
   Wish him well at parting.

So may God translate your soul
   Into peace eternal,
And the bliss of saints be yours
   In His realm supernal.

The second is a jovial *Song of the Open Road*, throbbing with the exhilaration of young life and madcap impudence. We must imagine that two vagabond students are drinking together before they part upon their several ways. One addresses the other as *frater catholice, vir apostolice*, vows to befriend him, and expounds the laws of loyalty which bind the brotherhood together. To the rest of the world they are a terror and a nuisance. Honest folk are jeeringly forbidden to beware of the *quadrivium*, which is apt to form a fourfold rogue instead of a scholar in four branches of knowledge.

The Latin metre is so light, careless, and airy, that I must admit an almost complete failure to do it justice in my English version. The refrain appears intended to imitate a bugle-call.

A SONG OF THE OPEN ROAD

No. 4

WE in our wandering,
　　Blithesome and squandering,
　　　　Tara, tantara, teino !

Eat to satiety,
Drink with propriety;
     Tara, tantara, teino!

Laugh till our sides we split,
Rags on our hides we fit;
     Tara, tantara, teino!

Jesting eternally,
Quaffing infernally:
     Tara, tantara, teino!

Craft's in the bone of us,
Fear 'tis unknown of us:
     Tara, tantara, teino!

When we're in neediness,
Thieve we with greediness:
     Tara, tantara, teino!

Brother catholical,
Man apostolical,
     Tara, tantara, teino!

Say what you will have done,
What you ask 'twill be done!
     Tara, tantara, teino!

Folk, fear the toss of the
Horns of philosophy!
>> Tara, tantara, teino!

Here comes a quadruple
Spoiler and prodigal!
>> Tara, tantara, teino!

License and vanity
Pamper insanity:
>> Tara, tantara, teino!

As the Pope bade us do,
Brother to brother's true:
>> Tara, tantara, teino!

Brother, best friend, adieu!
Now, I must part from you!
>> Tara, tantara, teino!

When will our meeting be?
Glad shall our greeting be!
>> Tara, tantara, teino!

Vows valedictory
Now have the victory;
>> Tara, tantara, teino!

> Clasped on each other's breast,
> Brother to brother pressed,
>   Tara, tantara, teino!

In the fourth place I insert the *Confession of Golias.*
This important composition lays bare the inner nature
of a Wandering Student, describing his vagrant habits,
his volatile and indiscriminate amours, his passion for
the dice-box, his devotion to wine, and the poetic
inspiration he was wont to draw from it.

In England this *Confession* was attributed to Walter
Map; and the famous drinking-song, on which the
Archdeacon of Oxford's reputation principally rests in
modern times, was extracted from the stanzas 11 *et
seq.*[1]   But, though Wright is unwilling to refuse Map
such honour as may accrue to his fame from the composition, we have little reason to regard it as his work.
The song was clearly written at Pavia—a point in-
explicably overlooked by Wright in the note appended
to stanza 9—and the Archbishop-elect of Cologne,
who is appealed to by name in stanza 24, was Reinald
von Dassel, a minister of Frederick Barbarossa.   This
circumstance enables us to determine the date of the
poem between 1162 and 1165.   When the *Confession*

[1] Wright's *Walter Mapes*, p. xlv.

was manipulated for English readers, *Praesul Covent-rensium, Praesul mihi cognite,* and *O pastor ecclesiae* were in several MS. redactions substituted for *Electe Coloniae.* Instead of *Papiae,* in stanza 8, we read *in mundo ;* but in stanza 9, where the rhyme required it, *Papiae* was left standing—a sufficient indication of literary rehandling by a clumsy scribe. In the text of the *Carmina Burana,* the *Confession* winds up with a petition that Reinald von Dassel should employ the poet as a secretary, or should bestow some mark of his bounty upon him.

THE CONFESSION OF GOLIAS

No. 5

BOILING in my spirit's veins
    With fierce indignation,
From my bitterness of soul
    Springs self-revelation :
Framed am I of flimsy stuff,
    Fit for levitation,
Like a thin leaf which the wind
    Scatters from its station.

While it is the wise man's part
   With deliberation
On a rock to base his heart's
   Permanent foundation,
With a running river I
   Find my just equation,
Which beneath the self-same sky
   Hath no habitation.

Carried am I like a ship
   Left without a sailor,
Like a bird that through the air
   Flies where tempests hale her;
Chains and fetters hold me not,
   Naught avails a jailer;
Still I find my fellows out
   Toper, gamester, railer.

To my mind all gravity
   Is a grave subjection;
Sweeter far than honey are
   Jokes and free affection.
All that Venus bids me do,
   Do I with erection,
For she ne'er in heart of man
   Dwelt with dull dejection.

Down the broad road do I run,
　　As the way of youth is ;
Snare myself in sin, and ne'er
　　Think where faith and truth is ,
Eager far for pleasure more
　　Than soul's health, the sooth is,
For this flesh of mine I care,
　　Seek not ruth where ruth is.

Prelate, most discreet of priests,
　　Grant me absolution !
Dear's the death whereof I die,
　　Sweet my dissolution ;
For my heart is wounded by
　　Beauty's soft suffusion ;
All the girls I come not nigh,
　　Mine are in illusion.

'Tis most arduous to make
　　Nature's self surrender ;
Seeing girls, to blush and be
　　Purity's defender !
We young men our longings ne'er
　　Shall to stern law render,
Or preserve our fancies from
　　Bodies smooth and tender.

Who, when into fire he falls,
　　Keeps himself from burning?
Who within Pavia's walls
　　Fame of chaste is earning?
Venus with her finger calls
　　Youths at every turning,
Snares them with her eyes, and thralls
　　With her amorous yearning.

If you brought Hippolitus
　　To Pavia Sunday,
He'd not be Hippolitus
　　On the following Monday;
Venus there keeps holiday
　　Every day as one day;
'Mid these towers in no tower dwells
　　Venus Verecunda.

In the second place I own
　　To the vice of gaming:
Cold indeed outside I seem,
　　Yet my soul is flaming:
But when once the dice-box hath
　　Stripped me to my shaming,
Make I songs and verses fit
　　For the world's acclaiming.

In the third place, I will speak
   Of the tavern's pleasure ;
For I never found nor find
   There the least displeasure ;
Nor shall find it till I greet
   Angels without measure,
Singing requiems for the souls
   In eternal leisure.

In the public-house to die
   Is my resolution ;
Let wine to my lips be nigh
   At life's dissolution :
That will make the angels cry,
   With glad elocution,
" Grant this toper, God on high,
   Grace and absolution ! "

With the cup the soul lights up,
   Inspirations flicker ;
Nectar lifts the soul on high
   With its heavenly ichor :
To my lips a sounder taste
   Hath the tavern's liquor
Than the wine a village clerk
   Waters for the vicar.

Nature gives to every man
   Some gift serviceable ;
Write I never could nor can
   Hungry at the table ;
Fasting, any stripling to
   Vanquish me is able ;
Hunger, thirst, I liken to
   Death that ends the fable.

Nature gives to every man
   Gifts as she is willing ;
I compose my verses when
   Good wine I am swilling,
Wine the best for jolly guest
   Jolly hosts are filling ;
From such wine rare fancies fine
   Flow like dews distilling.

Such my verse is wont to be
   As the wine I swallow ;
No ripe thoughts enliven me
   While my stomach's hollow ;
Hungry wits on hungry lips
   Like a shadow follow,
But when once I'm in my cups,
   I can beat Apollo.

Never to my spirit yet
  Flew poetic vision
Until first my belly had
  Plentiful provision ;
Let but Bacchus in the brain
  Take a strong position,
Then comes Phoebus flowing in
  With a fine precision.

There are poets, worthy men,
  Shrink from public places,
And in lurking-hole or den
  Hide their pallid faces ;
There they study, sweat, and woo
  Pallas and the Graces,
But bring nothing forth to view
  Worth the girls' embraces.

Fasting, thirsting, toil the bards,
  Swift years flying o'er them ;
Shun the strife of open life,
  Tumults of the forum ;
They, to sing some deathless thing,
  Lest the world ignore them,
Die the death, expend their breath,
  Drowned in dull decorum.

Lo! my frailties I've betrayed,
  Shown you every token,
Told you what your servitors
  Have against me spoken;
But of those men each and all
  Leave their sins unspoken,
Though they play, enjoy to-day.
  Scorn their pledges broken.

Now within the audience-room
  Of this blessèd prelate,
Sent to hunt out vice, and from
  Hearts of men expel it;
Let him rise, nor spare the bard,
  Cast at him a pellet:
He whose heart knows not crime's smart,
  Show my sin and tell it!

I have uttered openly
  All I knew that shamed me,
And have spued the poison forth
  That so long defamed me;
Of my old ways I repent,
  New life hath reclaimed me;
God beholds the heart—'twas man
  Viewed the face and blamed me.

Goodness now hath won my love,
    I am wroth with vices :
Made a new man in my mind,
    Lo, my soul arises !
Like a babe new milk I drink—
    Milk for me suffices,
Lest my heart should longer be
    Filled with vain devices.

Thou Elect of fair Cologne,
    Listen to my pleading !
Spurn not thou the penitent ;
    See, his heart is bleeding !
Give me penance ! what is due
    For my faults exceeding
I will bear with willing cheer,
    All thy precepts heeding.

Lo, the lion, king of beasts,
    Spares the meek and lowly ;
Toward submissive creatures he
    Tames his anger wholly.
Do the like, ye powers of earth,
    Temporal and holy !
Bitterness is more than's right
    When 'tis bitter solely.

XIV

Having been introduced to the worshipful order of vagrants both in their collective and in their personal capacity, we will now follow them to the woods and fields in spring. It was here that they sought love-adventures and took pastime after the restraints of winter.

The spring-songs are all, in the truest sense of the word, *lieder*—lyrics for music. Their affinities of form and rhythm are less with ecclesiastical verse than with the poetry of the Minnesinger and the Troubadour. Sometimes we are reminded of the French *pastourelle*, sometimes of the rustic ditty, with its monotonous refrain.

The exhilaration of the season which they breathe has something of the freshness of a lark's song, something at times of the richness of the nightingale's lament. The defect of the species may be indicated in a single phrase. It is a tedious reiteration of commonplaces in the opening stanzas. Here, however, is a lark-song.

WELCOME TO SPRING

No. 6

SPRING is coming! longed-for spring
    Now his joy discloses;
On his fair brow in a ring
    Bloom empurpled roses!
Birds are gay; how sweet their lay!
    Tuneful is the measure;
The wild wood grows green again,
Songsters change our winter's pain
    To a mirthful pleasure.

Now let young men gather flowers,
    On their foreheads bind them,
Maidens pluck them from the bowers,
    Then, when they have twined them,
Breathe perfume from bud and bloom,
    Where young love reposes,
And into the meadows so
All together laughing go,
    Crowned with ruddy roses.

Here again the nightingale's song, contending with
the young man's heart's lament of love, makes itself
heard.

THE LOVER AND THE NIGHTINGALE
No. 7

THESE hours of spring are jolly;
    Maidens, be gay!
Shake off dull melancholy,
    Ye lads, to-day!
    Oh! all abloom am I!
    It is a maiden love that makes me sigh,
    A new, new love it is wherewith I die!

The nightingale is singing
    So sweet a lay!
Her glad voice heavenward flinging—
    No check, no stay.

Flower of girls love-laden
    Is my sweetheart;
Of roses red the maiden
    For whom I smart.

The promise that she gives me
    Makes my heart bloom;
If she denies, she drives me
    Forth to the gloom.

My maid, to me relenting,
     Is fain for play;
Her pure heart, unconsenting,
     Saith, " Lover, stay! "

Hush, Philomel, thy singing,
     This little rest!
Let the soul's song rise ringing
     Up from the breast!

In desolate Decembers
     Man bides his time:
Spring stirs the slumbering embers;
     Love-juices climb.

Come, mistress, come, my maiden!
     Bring joy to me!
Come, come, thou beauty-laden!
     I die for thee!
     O all abloom am I!
It is a maiden love that makes me sigh,
A new, new love it is wherewith I die!

There is a very pretty *Invitation to Youth*, the refrain
of which, though partly undecipherable, seems to
indicate an Italian origin. I have thought it well to
omit this refrain; but it might be rendered thus,

maintaining the strange and probably corrupt reading
of the last line :—

> " List, my fair, list, *bela mia,*
> To the thousand charms of Venus !
> *Da hizevaleria.*"

THE INVITATION TO YOUTH
No. 8

TAKE your pleasure, dance and play,
Each with other while ye may :
Youth is nimble, full of grace ;
Age is lame, of tardy pace.

We the wars of love should wage,
Who are yet of tender age ;
'Neath the tents of Venus dwell
All the joys that youth loves well.

Young men kindle heart's desire ;
You may liken them to fire :
Old men frighten love away
With cold frost and dry decay.

A roundelay, which might be styled the *Praise of
May* or the exhortation to be liberal in love by *The
Example of the Rose*, shall follow.

THE EXAMPLE OF THE ROSE

No. 9

WINTER'S untruth yields at last,
    Spring renews old mother earth ;
Angry storms are overpast,
    Sunbeams fill the air with mirth ;
    Pregnant, ripening unto birth,
        All the world reposes.

Our delightful month of May,
    Not by birth, but by degree,
Took the first place, poets say ;
    Since the whole year's cycle he,
    Youngest, loveliest, leads with glee,
        And the cycle closes.

From the honours of the rose
    They decline, the rose abuse,
Who, when roses red unclose,
    Seek not their own sweets to use ;
    'Tis with largess, liberal dues,
        That the rose discloses.

Taught to wanton, taught to play,
By the young year's wanton flower,
We will take no heed to-day,
Have no thought for thrift this hour;
Thrift, whose uncongenial power
Laws on youth imposes.

Another song, blending the praises of spring with a
little pagan vow to Cupid, has in the original Latin a
distinction and purity of outline which might be almost
called Horatian.

THE VOW TO CUPID

No. 10

WINTER, now thy spite is spent,
Frost and ice and branches bent!
Fogs and furious storms are o'er,
Sloth and torpor, sorrow frore,
Pallid wrath, lean discontent.

Comes the graceful band of May!
Cloudless shines the limpid day,
Shine by night the Pleiades;
While a grateful summer breeze
Makes the season soft and gay.

Golden Love ! shine forth to view !
Souls of stubborn men subdue !
See me bend ! what is thy mind ?
Make the girl thou givest kind,
And a leaping ram's thy due !

O the jocund face of earth,
Breathing with young grassy birth
Every tree with foliage clad,
Singing birds in greenwood glad,
Flowering fields for lovers' mirth !

Nor is the next far below it in the same qualities of
neatness and artistic brevity.

A-MAYING.

No. 11

NOW the fields are laughing ; now the maids
Take their pastime ; laugh the leafy glades :
    Now the summer days are blooming,
      And the flowers their chaliced lamps for
        love illuming.

Fruit-trees blossom ; woods grow green again ;
Winter's rage is past : O ye young men,
    With the May-bloom shake off sadness !
    Love is luring you to join the maidens' gladness.

Let us then together sport and play ;
Cytherea bids the young be gay :
    Laughter soft and happy voices,
    Hope and love invite to mirth when May
      rejoices.

All the spring is in the lyric next upon my list.

THE RETURN OF SPRING

No. 12

SPRING returns, the glad new-comer,
    Bringing pleasure, banning pain :
Meadows bloom with early summer,
    And the sun shines out again :
All sad thoughts and passions vanish ;
Plenteous Summer comes to banish
    Winter with his starveling train.

Hails and snows and frosts together
   Melt and thaw like dews away ;
While the spring in cloudless weather
   Sucks the breast of jocund May;
Sad's the man and born for sorrow
Who can live not, dares not borrow
   Gladness from a summer's day.

Full of joy and jubilation,
   Drunk with honey of delight,
Are the lads whose aspiration
   Is the palm of Cupid's fight !
Youths, we'll keep the laws of Venus,
And with joy and mirth between us
   Live and love like Paris wight !

The next has the same accent of gladness, though it is tuned to a somewhat softer and more meditative note of feeling.

THE SWEETNESS OF THE SPRING

No. 13

VERNAL hours are sweet as clover,
  With love's honey running over;
Every heart on this earth burning
Finds new birth with spring's returning.

In the spring-time blossoms flourish,
Fields drink moisture, heaven's dews nourish;
Now the griefs of maidens, after
Dark days, turn to love and laughter.

Whoso love, are loved, together
Seek their pastime in spring weather;
And, with time and place agreeing,
Clasp, kiss, frolic, far from seeing.

Gradually the form of the one girl whom the lyrist
loves emerges from this wealth of description.

THE SUIT TO PHYLLIS

No. 14

HAIL ! thou longed-for month of May,
    Dear to lovers every day !
Thou that kindlest hour by hour
Life in man and bloom in bower !
O ye crowds of flowers and hues
That with joy the sense confuse,
Hail ! and to our bosom bring
Bliss and every jocund thing !
Sweet the concert of the birds ;
Lovers listen to their words :
For sad winter hath gone by,
And a soft wind blows on high.

Earth hath donned her purple vest,
Fields with laughing flowers are dressed,
Shade upon the wild wood spreads,
Trees lift up their leafy heads ;
Nature in her joy to-day
Bids all living things be gay ;
Glad her face and fair her grace
Underneath the sun's embrace !

Venus stirs the lover's brain,
With life's nectar fills his vein,
Pouring through his limbs the heat
Which makes pulse and passion beat.

O how happy was the birth
When the loveliest soul on earth
Took the form and life of thee,
Shaped in all felicity !
O how yellow is thy hair !
There is nothing wrong, I swear,
In the whole of thee ; thou art
Framed to fill a loving heart !
Lo, thy forehead queenly crowned,
And the eyebrows dark and round,
Curved like Iris at the tips,
Down the dark heavens when she slips !

Red as rose and white as snow
Are thy cheeks that pale and glow ;
'Mid a thousand maidens thou
Hast no paragon, I vow.
Round thy lips and red as be
Apples on the apple-tree ;
Bright thy teeth as any star ;
Soft and low thy speeches are ;

Long thy hand, and long thy side,
And the throat thy breasts divide;
All thy form beyond compare
Was of God's own art the care.

Sparks of passion sent from thee
Set on fire the heart of me;
Thee beyond all whom I know
I must love for ever so.
Lo, my heart to dust will burn
Unless thou this flame return;
Still the fire will last, and I,
Living now, at length shall die!
Therefore, Phyllis, hear me pray,
Let us twain together play,
Joining lip to lip and breast
Unto breast in perfect rest!

The lover is occasionally bashful, sighing at a distance.

MODEST LOVE

No. 15

SUMMER sweet is coming in;
Now the pleasant days begin;
Phoebus rules the earth at last;
For sad winter's reign is past.

Wounded with the love alone
Of one girl, I make my moan:
Grief pursues me till she bend
Unto me and condescend.

Take thou pity on my plight!
With my heart thy heart unite!
In my love thy own love blending,
Finding thus of life the ending!

Occasionally his passion assumes a romantic tone, as
is the case with the following *Serenade* to a girl called
Flos-de-spina in the Latin. Whether that was her
real name, or was only used for poetical purposes, does
not admit of debate now. Anyhow, Flos-de-spina,
Fior-di-spina, Fleur-d'épine, and English Flower-o'-
the-thorn are all of them pretty names for a girl.

THE SERENADE TO FLOWER-
O'-THE-THORN

No. 16

THE blithe young year is upward steering,
   Wild winter dwindles, disappearing;
The short, short days are growing longer,
Rough weather yields and warmth is stronger.
      Since January dawned, my mind
      Waves hither, thither, love-inclined
      For one whose will can loose or bind.

Prudent and very fair the maiden,
Than rose or lily more love-laden;
Stately of stature, lithe and slender,
There's naught so exquisite and tender.
      The Queen of France is not so dear;
      Death to my life comes very near
      If Flower-o'-the-thorn be not my cheer.

The Queen of Love my heart is killing
With her gold arrow pain-distilling;
The God of Love with torches burning
Lights pyre on pyre of ardent yearning.

> She is the girl for whom I'd die ;
> I want none dearer, far or nigh,
> Though grief on grief upon me lie.

> I with her love am thralled and taken,
> Whose flower doth flower, bud, bloom, and waken ;
> Sweet were the labour, light the burden,
> Could mouth kiss mouth for wage and guerdon.
>   No touch of lips my wound can still,
>   Unless two hearts grow one, one will,
>   One longing !   Flower of flowers, farewell !

Once at least we find him writing in absence to his mistress, and imploring her fidelity. This ranks among the most delicate in sentiment of the whole series.

THE LOVE-LETTER IN SPRING

No. 17

NOW the sun is streaming,
    Clear and pure his ray ;
April's glad face beaming
    On our earth to-day.

Unto love returneth
  Every gentle mind;
And the boy-god burneth
  Jocund hearts to bind.

All this budding beauty,
  Festival array,
Lays on us the duty
  To be blithe and gay.
Trodden ways are known, love!
  And in this thy youth,
To retain thy own love
  Were but faith and truth.

In faith love me solely,
  Mark the faith of me,
From thy whole heart wholly,
  From the soul of thee.
At this time of bliss, dear,
  I am far away;
Those who love like this, dear,
  Suffer every day!

At one time he seems upon the point of clasping his
felicity.

A SPRING DITTY

No. 18

IN the spring, ah happy day!
Underneath a leafy spray
With her sister stands my may.
    O sweet love!
        He who now is reft of thee
        Poor is he!

Ah, the trees, how fair they flower
Birds are singing in the bower;
Maidens feel of love the power.
    O sweet love!

See the lilies, how they blow!
And the maidens row by row
Praise the best of gods below.
    O sweet love!

If I held my sweetheart now,
In the wood beneath the bough,
I would kiss her, lip and brow.

O sweet love !
He who now is reft of thee,
Poor is he !

At another time he has clasped it, but he trembles
lest it should escape him.

LOVE-DOUBTS

No. 19

WITH so sweet a promise given
All my bosom burneth ;
Hope uplifts my heart to heaven,
Yet the doubt returneth,
Lest perchance that hope should be
Crushed and shattered suddenly.

On one girl my fancy so,
On one star, reposes ;
Her sweet lips with honey flow
And the scent of roses :
In her smile I laugh, and fire
Fills me with her love's desire.

Love in measure over-much
    Strikes man's soul with anguish ;
Anxious love's too eager touch
    Makes man fret and languish :
Thus in doubt and grief I pine ;
Pain more sure was none than mine.

Burning in love's fiery flood,
    Lo, my life is wasted !
Such the fever of my blood
    That I scarce have tasted
Mortal bread and wine, but sup
Like a god love's nectar-cup.

The village dance forms an important element in
the pleasures of the season.   Here is a pretty picture
in two stanzas of a linden sheltering some Suabian
meadow.

THE VILLAGE DANCE

No. 20

WIDE the lime-tree to the air
    Spreads her boughs and foliage fair ;
Thyme beneath is growing

On the verdant meadow where
   Dancers' feet are going.

Through the grass a little spring
Runs with jocund murmuring;
   All the place rejoices;
Cooling zephyrs breathe and sing
   With their summer voices.

I have freely translated a second, which presents a
more elaborate picture of a similar scene.

LOVE AMONG THE MAIDENS

No. 21

YONDER choir of virgins see
   Through the spring advancing,
Where the sun's warmth, fair and free,
   From the green leaves glancing,
Weaves a lattice of light gloom
   And soft sunbeams o'er us,
'Neath the linden-trees in bloom,
   For the Cyprian chorus.

In this vale where blossoms blow,
   Blooming, summer-scented,
'Mid the lilies row by row,
   Spreads a field flower-painted.
Here the blackbirds through the dale
   Each to each are singing,
And the jocund nightingale
   Her fresh voice is flinging.

See the maidens crowned with rose
   Sauntering through the grasses!
Who could tell the mirth of those
   Laughing, singing lasses?
Or with what a winning grace
   They their charms discover,
Charms of form and blushing face,
   To the gazing lover?

Down the flowery greenwood glade
   As I chanced to wander,
From bright eyes a serving-maid
   Shot Love's arrows yonder;
I for her, 'mid all the crew
   Of the girls of Venus,
Wait and yearn until I view
   Love spring up between us.

Another lyric of complicated rhyming structure introduces a not dissimilar motive, with touches that seem, in like manner, to indicate its German origin. It may be remarked that the lover's emotion has here unusual depth, a strain of *sehnsucht;* and the picture of the mother followed by her daughter in the country-dance suggests the domesticity of Northern races.

AT THE VILLAGE DANCE

No. 22

MEADOWS bloom, in Winter's room
    Reign the Loves and Graces,
With their gift of buds that lift
    Bright and laughing faces;
'Neath the ray of genial May,
    Shining, glowing, blushing, growing,
    They the joys of spring are showing
In their manifold array.

Song-birds sweet the season greet,
    Tune their merry voices;
Sound the ways with hymns of praise,
    Every lane rejoices.

On the bough in greenwood now
   Flowers are springing, perfumes flinging,
   While young men and maids are clinging
To the loves they scarce avow.

O'er the grass together pass
   Bands of lads love-laden:
Row by row in bevies go
   Bride and blushing maiden.
See with glee 'neath linden-tree,
   Where the dancing girls are glancing,
   How the matron is advancing!
At her side her daughter see!

She's my own, for whom alone,
   If fate wills, I'll tarry;
Young May-moon, or late or soon,
   'Tis with her I'd marry!
Now with sighs I watch her rise,
   She the purely loved, the surely
   Chosen, who my heart securely
Turns from grief to Paradise.

In her sight with heaven's own light
   Like the gods I blossom;
Care for nought till she be brought
   Yielding to my bosom.

Thirst divine my soul doth pine
   To behold her and enfold her,
   With clasped arms alone to hold her
In Love's holy hidden shrine.

But the theme of the dance is worked up with even greater elaboration and a more studied ingenuity of rhyme and rhythm in the following characteristic song. This has the true accent of what may be called the *Musa Vagabundula*, and is one of the best lyrics of the series :—

INVITATION TO THE DANCE

No. 23

CAST aside dull books and thought;
   Sweet is folly, sweet is play :
Take the pleasure Spring hath brought
   In youth's opening holiday !
Right it is old age should ponder
   On grave matters fraught with care ;
Tender youth is free to wander,
   Free to frolic light as air.

> Like a dream our prime is flown,
>   Prisoned in a study :
> Sport and folly are youth's own,
>   Tender youth and ruddy.

Lo, the Spring of life slips by,
    Frozen Winter comes apace ;
Strength is 'minished silently,
    Care writes wrinkles on our face :
Blood dries up and courage fails us,
    Pleasures dwindle, joys decrease,
Till old age at length assails us
    With his troop of illnesses.

> Like a dream our prime is flown,
>   Prisoned in a study ;
> Sport and folly are youth's own,
>   Tender youth and ruddy.

Live we like the gods above ;
    This is wisdom, this is truth :
Chase the joys of tender love
    In the leisure of our youth !
Keep the vows we swore together,
    Lads, obey that ordinance ;
Seek the fields in sunny weather,
    Where the laughing maidens dance.

Like a dream our prime is flown,
  Prisoned in a study;
Sport and folly are youth's own,
  Tender youth and ruddy.

There the lad who lists may see
  Which among the maids is kind:
There young limbs deliciously
  Flashing through the dances wind:
While the girls their arms are raising,
  Moving, winding o'er the lea,
Still I stand and gaze, and gazing
  They have stolen the soul of me!
    Like a dream our prime is flown,
      Prisoned in a study;
    Sport and folly are youth's own,
      Tender youth and ruddy.

XV

A separate Section can be devoted to songs in the
manner of the early French pastoral. These were
fashionable at a remote period in all parts of Europe;
and I have already had occasion, in another piece of
literary history, to call attention to the Italian madrigals

of the fourteenth century composed in this species.[1]
Their point is mainly this : A man of birth and edu-
cation, generally a dweller in the town, goes abroad
into the fields, lured by fair spring weather, and makes
love among trees to a country wench.

The *Vagi* turn the pastoral to their own purpose,
and always represent the greenwood lover as a *clericus*.
One of these rural pieces has a pretty opening stanza :—

> " When the sweet Spring was ascending,
>   Not yet May, at April's ending,
>   While the sun was heavenward wending,
>   Stood a girl of grace transcending
>   Underneath the green bough, sending
>   Songs aloft with pipings. "

Another gives a slightly comic turn to the chief
incident.

A PASTORAL

No. 24

THERE went out in the dawning light
        A little rustic maiden ;
Her flock so white, her crook so slight,
    With fleecy new wool laden.

[1] See *Renaissance in Italy*, vol. iv. p. 156.

Small is the flock, and there you'll see
   The she-ass and the wether ;
This goat's a he, and that's a she,
   The bull-calf and the heifer.

She looked upon the green sward, where
   A student lay at leisure :
" What do you there, young sir, so fair ? "
   " Come, play with me, my treasure ! "

A third seems to have been written in the South, perhaps upon the shores of one of the Italian lakes—Como or Garda.

THE MULBERRY-GATHERER

No. 25

IN the summer's burning heat,
   When the flowers were blooming sweet,
I had chosen, as 'twas meet,
'Neath an olive bough my seat ;
Languid with the glowing day,
Lazy, careless, apt for play.

Stood the tree in fields where grew
Painted flowers of every hue,

Grass that flourished with the dew,
Fresh with shade where breezes blew;
Plato, with his style so rare,
Could not paint a spot more fair.

Runs a babbling brook hard by,
Chants the nightingale on high;
Water-nymphs with song reply.
"Sure, 'tis Paradise," I cry;
For I know not any place
Of a sweeter, fresher grace.

While I take my solace here,
And in solace find good cheer,
Shade from summer, coolness dear,
Comes a shepherd maiden near—
Fairer, sure, there breathes not now—
Plucking mulberries from the bough.

Seeing her, I loved her there:
Venus did the trick, I'll swear!
"Come, I am no thief, to scare,
Rob, or murder unaware;
I and all I have are thine,
Thou than Flora more divine!"

But the girl made answer then :
"Never played I yet with men ;
Cruel to me are my kin :
My old mother scolds me when
In some little thing I stray :—
Hold, I prithee, sir, to-day ! "

A fourth, consisting of a short conventional introduction in praise of Spring, followed by a dialogue
between a young man and a girl, in which the metre
changes for the last two stanzas, may be classed among
the pastorals, although it is a somewhat irregular
example of the species.

THE WOOING

No. 26

ALL the woods are now in flower,
   Song-birds sing in field and bower,
Orchards their white blossoms shower :
Lads, make merry in Love's hour !

Sordid grief hath flown away,
Fervid Love is here to-day ;

He will tame without delay
Those who love not while they may.

He. " Fairest maiden, list to me ;
Do not thus disdainful be ;
Scorn and anger disagree
With thy youth, and injure thee.

I am weaker than thou art ;
Mighty Love hath pierced my heart ;
Scarce can I endure his dart :
Lest I die, heal, heal my smart ! "

She. " Why d' you coax me, suitor blind ?
What you seek you will not find ;
I'm too young for love to bind ;
Such vain trifles vex my mind.

Is't your will with me to toy ?
I'll not mate with man or boy :
Like the Phœnix, to enjoy
Single life shall be my joy."

He. " Yet Love is tyrannous,
Harsh, fierce, imperious !
He who man's heart can thus
   Shatter, may make to bow
   Maidens as stern as thou ! "

She. " Now by your words I'm 'ware
What you wish, what you are ;
You know love well, I swear !
So I'll be loved by you ;
Now I'm on fire too ! "

XVI

Some semi-descriptive pieces, which connect the songs of Spring with lyrics of a more purely personal emotion, can boast of rare beauty in the original.

The most striking of these, upon the theme of Sleep and Love, I have tried to render in trochaic verse, feeling it impossible, without knowledge of the medieval melody, to reproduce its complicated and now only half-intelligible rhythms.

A DESCANT UPON SLEEP AND LOVE

No. 27

WHEN the lamp of Cynthia late
Rises in her silver state,
Through her brother's roseate light,
Blushing on the brows of night ;

Then the pure ethereal air
Breathes with zephyr blowing fair;
Clouds and vapours disappear.
As with chords of lute or lyre,
Soothed the spirits now respire,
And the heart revives again
Which once more for love is fain.
But the orient evening star
Sheds with influence kindlier far
Dews of sweet sleep on the eye
Of o'er-tired mortality.

Oh, how blessed to take and keep
Is the antidote of sleep!
Sleep that lulls the storms of care
And of sorrow unaware,
Creeping through the closèd doors
Of the eyes, and through the pores
Breathing bliss so pure and rare
That with love it may compare.

Then the god of dreams doth bring
To the mind some restful thing,
Breezes soft that rippling blow
O'er ripe cornfields row by row,

Murmuring rivers round whose brim
Silvery sands the swallows skim,
Or the drowsy circling sound
Of old mill-wheels going round,
Which with music steal the mind
And the eyes in slumber bind.

When the deeds of love are done
Which bland Venus had begun,
Languor steals with pleasant strain
Through the chambers of the brain,
Eyes 'neath eyelids gently tired
Swim and seek the rest desired.
How deliciously at last
Into slumber love hath passed!
But how sweeter yet the way
Which leads love again to play!

From the soothed limbs upward spread
Glides a mist divinely shed,
Which invades the heart and head ·
Drowsily it veils the eyes,
Bending toward sleep's paradise,
And with curling vapour round
Fills the lids, the senses swound,
Till the visual ray is bound

By those ministers which make
Life renewed in man awake.

Underneath the leafy shade
Of a tree in quiet laid,
While the nightingale complains
Singing of her ancient pains,
Sweet it is still hours to pass,
But far sweeter on the grass
With a buxom maid to play
All a summer's holiday.
When the scent of herb and flower
Breathes upon the silent hour,
When the rose with leaf and bloom
Spreads a couch of pure perfume,
Then the grateful boon of sleep
Falls with satisfaction deep,
Showering dews our eyes above,
Tired with honeyed strife of love.

In how many moods the mind
Of poor lovers, weak and blind,
Wavers like the wavering wind!
As a ship in darkness lost,
Without anchor tempest-tossed,

So with hope and fear imbued
It roams in great incertitude
Love's tempestuous ocean-flood.

A portion of this descant finds an echo in another
lyric of the *Carmina Burana* :—

" With young leaves the wood is new;
    Now the nightingale is singing;
And field-flowers of every hue
    On the sward their bloom are flinging.
Sweet it is to brush the dew
    From wild lawns and woody places!
Sweeter yet to wreathe the rose
    With the lily's virgin graces;
But the sweetest sweet man knows,
    Is to woo a girl's embraces."

The most highly wrought of descriptive poems in
this species is the *Dispute of Flora and Phyllis*, which
occurs both in the *Carmina Burana* and in the English
MSS. edited by Wright. The motive of the composition is as follows:—Two girls wake in the early
morning, and go out to walk together through the fields.
Each of them is in love; but Phyllis loves a soldier,
Flora loves a scholar. They interchange confidences,
the one contending with the other for the superiority
of her own sweetheart.

Having said so much, I will present the first part of
the poem in the English version I have made.

FLORA AND PHYLLIS

Part I

No. 28

IN the spring-time, when the skies
   Cast off winter's mourning,
And bright flowers of every hue
   Earth's lap are adorning,
At the hour when Lucifer
   Gives the stars their warning,
Phyllis woke, and Flora too,
   In the early morning.

Both the girls were fain to go
   Forth in sunny weather,
For love-laden bosoms throw
   Sleep off like a feather;
Then with measured steps and slow
   To the fields together
Went they, seeking pastime new
   'Mid the flowers and heather.

Both were virgins, both, I ween,
　　Were by birth princesses ;
Phyllis let her locks flow free,
　　Flora trained her tresses.
Not like girls they went, but like
　　Heavenly holinesses ;
And their faces shone like dawn
　　'Neath the day's caresses.

Equal beauty, equal birth,
　　These fair maidens mated ;
Youthful were the years of both,
　　And their minds elated ;
Yet they were a pair unpaired,
　　Mates by strife unmated ;
For one loved a clerk, and one
　　For a knight was fated.

Naught there was of difference
　　'Twixt them to the seeing,
All alike, within without,
　　Seemed in them agreeing ;
With one garb, one cast of mind,
　　And one mode of being,
Only that they could not love
　　Save with disagreeing.

In the tree-tops overhead
  A spring breeze was blowing,
And the meadow lawns around
  With green grass were growing;
Through the grass a rivulet
  From the hill was flowing,
Lively, with a pleasant sound
  Garrulously going.

That the girls might suffer less
  From the noon resplendent,
Near the stream a spreading pine
  Rose with stem ascendant;
Crowned with boughs and leaves aloft,
  O'er the fields impendent;
From all heat on every hand
  Airily defendent.

On the sward the maidens sat,
  Naught that seat surpasses;
Phyllis near the rivulet,
  Flora 'mid the grasses;
Each into the chamber sweet
  Of her own soul passes,
Love divides their thoughts, and wounds
  With his shafts the lasses.

Love within the breast of each,
　　Hidden, unsuspected,
Lurks and draws forth sighs of grief
　　From their hearts dejected :
Soon their ruddy cheeks grow pale,
　　Conscious, love-affected ;
Yet their passion tells no tale,
　　By soft shame protected.

Phyllis now doth overhear
　　Flora softly sighing :
Flora with like luck detects
　　Sigh to sigh replying.
Thus the girls exchange the game,
　　Each with other vying ;
Till the truth leaps out at length,
　　Plain beyond denying.

Long this interchange did last
　　Of mute conversation ;
All of love-sighs fond and fast
　　Was that dissertation.
Love was in their minds, and Love
　　Made their lips his station ;
Phyllis then, while Flora smiled,
　　Opened her oration.

" Soldier brave, my love ! " she said,
  " Where is now my Paris ?
Fights he in the field, or where
  In the wide world tarries ?
Oh, the soldier's life, I swear,
  All life's glory carries ;
Only valour clothed in arms
  With Dame Venus marries ! "

Phyllis thus opens the question whether a soldier or
a scholar be the fitter for love.   Flora responds, and
for some time they conduct the dispute in true scholastic
fashion.   Being unable to settle it between themselves,
they resolve to seek out Love himself, and to refer the
matter to his judgment.   One girl mounts a mule, the
other a horse ; and these are no ordinary animals, for
Neptune reared one beast as a present to Venus, Vulcan
forged the metal-work of bit and saddle, Minerva
embroidered the trappings, and so forth.   After a short
journey they reach the Garden of Love, which is
described with a truly luxuriant wealth of imagery
It resembles some of the earlier Renaissance pictures,
especially one of great excellence by a German artist
which I once saw in a dealer's shop at Venice, and
which ought now to grace a public gallery.

FLORA AND PHYLLIS

PART III

No. 29

ON their steeds the ladies ride,
  Two fair girls and slender;
Modest are their eyes and mild,
  And their cheeks are tender.
Thus young lilies break the sheath,
  Budding roses render
Blushes, and twinned pairs of stars
  Climb the heavens with splendour.

Toward Love's Paradise they fare,
  Such, I ween, their will is;
While the strife between the pair
  Turns their cheeks to lilies;
Phyllis Flora flouts, and fair
  Flora flouteth Phyllis;
Flora's hand a hawk doth bear,
  And a goshawk Phyllis.

After a short space they came
  Where a grove was growing;
At the entrance of the same
  Rills with murmur flowing;

There the wind with myrrh and spice
  Redolent was blowing,
Sounds of timbrel, harp, and lyre
  Through the branches going.

All the music man could make
  There they heard in plenty;
Timbrel, psaltery, lyre, and lute,
  Harp and viol dainty;
Voices that in part-song meet
  Choiring forte, lente;
Sounds the diatesseron,
  Sounds the diapente.

All the tongues of all the birds
  With full cry were singing;
There the blackbird's melody
  Sweet and true was ringing;
Wood-dove, lark, and thrush on high
  Jocund anthems flinging,
With the nightingale, who still
  To her grief was clinging.

When the girls drew nigh the grove,
  Some fear came upon them;
Further as they fared, the charm
  Of the pleasance won them;

All the birds so sweetly sang
　　That a spell was on them,
And their bosoms warmed with love
　　At the welcome shown them.

Man would be immortal if
　　He could there be dwelling:
Every branch on every tree
　　With ripe fruit is swelling;
All the ways with nard and myrrh
　　And with spice are smelling:
How divine the Master is
　　All the house is telling.

Blithesome bands arrest their gaze,
　　Youths and maidens dancing;
Bodies beauteous as the stars,
　　Eyes with heaven's light glancing;
And the bosoms of the girls,
　　At the sight entrancing,
Leap to view such marvels new,
　　Joy with joy enhancing!

They their horses check, and light,
　　Moved with sudden pleasure;
Half forget what brought them here,
　　Thralled by love and leisure;

Till once more the nightingale
    Tuned her thrilling measure;
At that cry each girl again
    Hugs her hidden treasure.

Round the middle of the grove
    Was a place enchanted,
Which the god for his own rites
    Specially had planted;
Fauns and nymphs and satyrs here
    Flowery alleys haunted,
And before the face of Love
    Played and leaped and chaunted.

In their hands they carry thyme,
    Crowns of fragrant roses;
Bacchus leads the choir divine
    And the dance composes;
Nymphs and fauns with feet in tune
    Interchange their posies;
But Silenus trips and reels
    When the chorus closes.

On an ass the elder borne
    All the mad crew guideth;
Mirth and laughter at the view
    Through Love's glad heart glideth

" Io ! " shouts the eld ; that sound
 In his throat subsideth,
For his voice in wine is drowned,
 And his old age chideth.

'Mid these pleasant sights appears
 Love, the young joy-giver ;
Bright as stars his eyes, and wings
 On his shoulders shiver ;
In his left hand is the bow,
 At his side the quiver ;
From his state the world may know
 He is lord for ever.

Leans the boy upon a staff
 Intertwined with flowers,
Scent of nectar from his hair
 Breathes around the bowers ;
Hand in hand before him kneel
 Three celestial Hours,
Graces who Love's goblet fill
 From immortal showers.

It would surely be superfluous to point out the fluent
elegance of this poem, or to dwell farther upon the
astonishing fact that anything so purely Renaissance in
tone should have been produced in the twelfth century.

Cupid, as was natural, settles the dispute of the two girls by deciding that scholars are more suitable for love than soldiers.

This would be the place to introduce another long descriptive poem, if the nature of its theme rendered it fit for translation. It relates the visit of a student to what he calls the *Templum Veneris;* in other words, to the house of a courtesan. Her attendants are sirens; and the whole poem, dealing with a vulgar incident, is conducted in this mock-heroic strain.[1]

XVII

We pass now to love-poems of a more purely personal kind. One of these, which is too long for translation and in some respects ill-suited to a modern taste, forms the proper transition from the descriptive to the lyrical section. It starts with phrases culled from hymns to the Virgin :—

> "Si linguis angelicis
> Loquar et humanis."

> "Ave formosissima,
> Gemma pretiosa;
> Ave decus virginum,
> Virgo gloriosa!"

---

[1] *Carmina Burana,* p. 138.

These waifs and strays of religious diction are
curiously blent with romantic and classical allusions.
The girl is addressed in the same breath as—

> " Blanziflor et Helena,
> Venus generosa."

Toward the close of the poem, the lover, who at
length has reached the object of his heart's desire,
breaks into this paean of victorious passion :—

> "What more ? Around the maiden's neck
>   My arms I flung with yearning ;
> Upon her lips I gave and took
>   A thousand kisses burning :
> Again and yet again I cried,
>   With whispered vows and sighing,
> This, this alone, sure, sure it was
>   For which my heart was dying !
>
> Who is the man that does not know
>   The sweets that followed after ?
> My former pains, my sobs and woe,
>   Were changed for love and laughter :
> The joys of Paradise were ours
>   In overflowing measure ;
> We tasted every shape of bliss
>   And every form of pleasure."

The next piece which I shall quote differs in some
important respects from the general style adopted by
the Goliardi in their love-poetry. It is written in

rhyming or leonine hexameters, and is remarkable for its quaint play on names, conceived and executed in a truly medieval taste.

FLOS FLORAE

No. 30

TAKE thou this rose, O Rose! the loves in the
  rose repose:
I with love of the rose am caught at the winter's close:
Take thou this flower, my flower, and cherish it in
  thy bower:
Thou in thy beauty's power shalt lovelier blow each
  hour:
Gaze at the rose, and smile, my rose, in mine eyes the
  while:
To thee the roses belong, thy voice is the nightingale's
  song:
Give thou the rose a kiss, it blushes like thy mouth's
  bliss:
Flowers in a picture seem not flowers, but flowers in a
  dream:
Who paints the rose's bloom, paints not the rose's
  perfume.

In complete contrast to this conceited and euphuistic style of composition stands a slight snatch of rustic melody, consisting of little but reiteration and refrain.

A BIRD'S SONG OF LOVE

No. 31

COME to me, O come!
Let me not die, but come!
    Hyria hysria nazaza
      Trillirivos.

Fair is thy face, O fair!
Fair thine eyes, O how fair!
    Hyria hysria nazaza
      Trillirivos.

Fair is thy flowing hair!
O fair, O fair, how fair!
    Hyria hysria nazaza
      Trillirivos.

Redder than rose art thou,
Whiter than lily thou!
    Hyria hysria nazaza
      Trillirivos.

Fairer than all, I vow,
Ever my pride art thou !
        Hyria hysria nazaza
            Trillirivos.

The following displays an almost classical intensity
of voluptuous passion, and belongs in all probability to a
period later than the *Carmina Burana*.   I have ventured,
in translating it, to borrow the structure of a song which
occurs in Fletcher's *Rollo* (act v. scene 2), the first
stanza of which is also found in Shakespeare's *Measure
for Measure* (act iv. scene 1), and to insert one or two
phrases from Fletcher's version.   Whether the composer
of that song had ever met with the Latin lyric to Lydia
can scarcely form the subject of critical conjecture.   Yet
there is a faint evanescent resemblance between the two
poems.

TO LYDIA

No. 32

LYDIA bright, thou girl more white
    Than the milk of morning new,
Or young lilies in the light !
    Matched with thy rose-whiteness, hue

Of red rose or white rose pales,
And the polished ivory fails,
        Ivory fails.

Spread, O spread, my girl, thy hair,
   Amber-hued and heavenly bright,
As fine gold or golden air !
   Show, O show thy throat so white,
Throat and neck that marble fine
Over thy white breasts incline,
        Breasts incline.

Lift, O lift thine eyes that are
   Underneath those eyelids dark,
Lustrous as the evening star
   'Neath the dark heaven's purple arc !
Bare, O bare thy cheeks of rose,
Dyed with Tyrian red that glows,
        Red that glows.

Give, O give those lips of love
   That the coral boughs eclipse ;
Give sweet kisses, dove by dove,
   Soft descending on my lips.
See my soul how forth she flies !
'Neath each kiss my pierced heart dies,
        Pierced heart dies.

Wherefore dost thou draw my life,
   Drain my heart's blood with thy kiss?
Scarce can I endure the strife
   Of this ecstasy of bliss!
Set, O set my poor heart free,
Bound in icy chains by thee,
             Chains by thee.

Hide, O hide those hills of snow,
   Twinned upon thy breast that rise,
Where the virgin fountains flow
   With fresh milk of Paradise!
Thy bare bosom breathes of myrrh,
From thy whole self pleasures stir,
             Pleasures stir.

Hide, O hide those paps that tire
   Sense and spirit with excess
Of snow-whiteness and desire
   Of thy breast's deliciousness!
See'st thou, cruel, how I swoon?
Leav'st thou me half lost so soon?
             Lost so soon?

In rendering this lyric to Lydia, I have restored the
fifth stanza, only one line of which,

"Quid mihi sugis vivum sanguinem,"

remains in the original.   This I did because it seemed
necessary to effect the transition from the stanzas beginning *Pande, puella, pande,* to those beginning *Conde
papillas, conde.*

Among these more direct outpourings of personal
passion, place may be found for a delicate little *Poem
of Privacy,* which forms part of the *Carmina Burana.*
Unfortunately, the text of this slight piece is very
defective in the MS., and has had to be conjecturally
restored in several places.

A POEM OF PRIVACY

No. 33

WHEN a young man, passion-laden,
     In a chamber meets a maiden,
   Then felicitous communion,
By love's strain between the twain,
   Grows from forth their union ;
For the game, it hath no name,
Of lips, arms, and hidden charms.

Nor can I here forbear from inserting another *Poem
of Privacy,* bolder in its openness of speech, more

glowing in its warmth of colouring. If excuse should
be pleaded or the translation and reproduction of this
distinctly Pagan ditty, it must be found in the singularity
of its motive, which is as unmedieval as could be desired
by the bitterest detractor of medieval sentiment. We
seem, while reading it, to have before our eyes the
Venetian picture of a Venus, while the almost prosaic
particularity of description illustrates what I have said
above about the detailed realism of the Goliardic
style.

FLORA

No. 34

RUDELY blows the winter blast,
    Withered leaves are falling fast,
Cold hath hushed the birds at last.
    While the heavens were warm and glowing,
        Nature's offspring loved in May ;
    But man's heart no debt is owing
        To such change óf month or day
        As the dumb brute-beasts obey.
Oh, the joys of this possessing !
How unspeakable the blessing
        That my Flora yields to-day !

Labour long I did not rue,
Ere I won my wages due,
And the prize I played for drew.
  Flora with her brows of laughter,
    Gazing on me, breathing bliss,
  Draws my yearning spirit after,
    Sucks my soul forth in a kiss:
    Where's the pastime matched with this:
Oh, the joys of this possessing!
How unspeakable the blessing
    Of my Flora's loveliness!

Truly mine is no harsh doom,
While in this secluded room
Venus lights for me the gloom!
  Flora faultless as a blossom
    Bares her smooth limbs for mine eyes;
  Softly shines her virgin bosom,
    And the breasts that gently rise
    Like the hills of Paradise.
Oh, the joys of this possessing!
How unspeakable the blessing
    When my Flora is the prize!

From her tender breasts decline,
In a gradual curving line,

Flanks like swansdown white and fine.
    On her skin the touch discerneth
        Naught of rough ; 'tis soft as snow :
    'Neath the waist her belly turneth
        Unto fulness, where below
        In Love's garden lilies blow.
Oh, the joys of this possessing !
How unspeakable the blessing !
        Sweetest sweets from Flora flow

Ah ! should Jove but find my fair,
He would fall in love, I swear,
And to his old tricks repair :
    In a cloud of gold descending
        As on Danae's brazen tower,
    Or the sturdy bull's back bending,
        Or would veil his godhood's power
        In a swan's form for one hour.
Oh, the joys of this possessing !
How unspeakable the blessing !
        How divine my Flora's flower !

A third " poem of privacy " may be employed to
temper this too fervid mood. I conceive it to be
meant for the monologue of a lover in the presence of

his sweetheart, and to express the varying lights and shades of his emotion.

THE LOVER'S MONOLOGUE
No. 35

LOVE rules everything that is :
Love doth change hearts in a kiss :
Love seeks devious ways of bliss :
Love than honey sweeter,
Love than gall more bitter.
Blind Love hath no modesties.
Love is lukewarm, fiery, cold ;
Love is timid, overbold ;
Loyal, treacherous, manifold.

Present time is fit for play :
Let Love find his mate to-day :
Hark, the birds, how sweet their lay !
Love rules young men wholly ;
Love lures maidens solely.
Woe to old folk ! sad are they.
Sweetest woman ever seen,
Fairest, dearest, is my queen ;
And alas ! my chiefest teen.

Let an old man, chill and drear,
Never come thy bosom near ;
Oft he sleeps with sorry cheer,
    Too cold to delight thee :
    Naught could less invite thee.
Youth with youth must mate, my dear
  Blest the union I desire ;
  Naught I know and naught require,
  Better than to be thy squire.

Love flies all the world around :
Love in wanton wiles is wound :
Therefore youth and maid are bound
    In Love's fetters duly.
    She is joyless truly
Who no lover yet hath found !
  All the night in grief and smart
  She must languish, wear her heart ;
  Bitter is that woman's part.

Love is simple, Love is sly ;
Love is pale, of ruddy dye :
Love is all things, low and high .
    Love is serviceable,
    Constant and unstable :
Love obeys Art's empery.

In this closed room Love takes flight,
In the silence of the night,
Love made captive, conquered quite.

The next is singularly, quaintly musical in the
original, but for various reasons I have not been able to
adhere exactly to its form.   I imagine that it is the
work of the same poet who composed the longer piece
which I shall give immediately after.   Both are
addressed to Caecilia ; I have used the name Phyllis
in my version.

THE INVITATION TO LOVE

No. 36

LIST, my girl, with words I woo ;
Lay not wanton hands on you :
Sit before you, in your face
Gazing, ah ! and seeking grace :
Fix mine eyes, nor let them rove
From the mark where shafts of love
          Their flight wing.
Try, my girl, O try what bliss
Young men render when they kiss !

Youth is alway sturdy, straight ;
Old age totters in its gait.
These delights of love we bring
Have the suppleness of spring,
Softness, sweetness, wantoning ;
Clasp, my Phyllis, in their ring
Sweeter sweets than poets sing,
   Anything and everything !

After daytime's heat from heaven
Dews on thirsty fields are given ;
After verdant leaf and stem
Shoots the white flower's diadem ;
After the white flower's bloom
To the night their faint perfume
   Lilies fling.
  Try, my girl, etc., *da capo*.

The poem, *Ludo cum Caecilia*, which comes next in
order, is one of the most perfect specimens of Goliardic
writing. To render its fluent, languid, and yet airy
grace, in any language but the Latin, is, I think, impossible. Who could have imagined that the subtlety,
the refinement, almost the perversity of feeling expressed
in it, should have been proper to a student of the
twelfth century ? The poem is spoiled toward its

close by astrological and grammatical conceits; and
the text is corrupt.   That part I have omitted,
together with some stanzas which offend a modern
taste.

PHYLLIS

No. 37

THINK no evil, have no fear,
    If I play with Phyllis;
I am but the guardian dear
    Of her girlhood's lilies,
Lest too soon her bloom should swoon
    Like spring's daffodillies.

All I care for is to play,
    Gaze upon my treasure,
Now and then to touch her hand,
    Kiss in modest measure;
But the fifth act of love's game,
    Dream not of that pleasure!

For to touch the bloom of youth
    Spoils its frail complexion;
Let the young grape gently grow
    Till it reach perfection;

Hope within my heart doth glow
  Of the girl's affection.

Sweet above all sweets that are
  'Tis to play with Phyllis;
For her thoughts are white as snow,
  In her heart no ill is;
And the kisses that she gives
  Sweeter are than lilies.

Love leads after him the gods
  Bound in pliant traces;
Harsh and stubborn hearts he bends,
  Breaks with blows of maces;
Nay, the unicorn is tamed
  By a girl's embraces.

Love leads after him the gods,
  Jupiter with Juno;
To his waxen measure treads
  Masterful Neptune O!
Pluto stern to souls below
  Melts to this one tune O!

Whatsoe'er the rest may do,
  Let us then be playing:

> Take the pastime that is due
>   While we're yet a-Maying;
> I am young and young are you;
>   'Tis the time for playing.

Up to this time, the happiness of love returned and satisfied has been portrayed. The following lyric exhibits a lover pining at a distance, soothing his soul with song, and indulging in visions of happiness beyond his grasp—εἰδώλοις κάλλευς κῶφα χλιαινόμενος, as Meleager phrased it on a similar occasion

LOVE LONGINGS

No. 38

WITH song I seek my fate to cheer,
   As doth the swan when death draws near;
Youth's roses from my cheeks retire,
My heart is worn with fond desire.
      Since care and woe increase and grow, while
         light burns low,
            Poor wretch I die!
      Heigho! I die, poor wretch I die!
Constrained to love, unloved; such luck have I!

If she could love me whom I love,
I would not then exchange with Jove:
Ah! might I clasp her once, and drain
Her lips as thirsty flowers drink rain!
　　With death to meet, his welcome greet, from
　　　　life retreat,
　　　　　　I were full fain!
　　Heigho! full fain, I were full fain,
Could I such joy, such wealth of pleasure gain!

When I bethought me of her breast,
Those hills of snow my fancy pressed;
Longing to touch them with my hand,
Love's laws I then did understand.
　　Rose of the south, blooms on her mouth; I
　　　　felt love's drouth
　　　　　　That mouth to kiss!
　　Heigho! to kiss, that mouth to kiss!
Lost in day-dreams and vain desires of bliss.

The next is the indignant repudiation by a lover
of the calumny that he has proved unfaithful to his
mistress. The strongly marked double rhymes of the
original add peculiar vehemence to his protestations;
while the abundance of cheap mythological allusions is
emphatically Goliardic.

THE LOVER'S VOW

No. 39

FALSE the tongue and foul with slander,
Poisonous treacherous tongue of pander,
Tongue the hangman's knife should sever,
Tongue in flames to burn for ever;

Which hath called me a deceiver,
Faithless lover, quick to leave her,
Whom I love, and leave her slighted,
For another, unrequited!

Hear, ye Muses nine! nay, rather,
Jove, of gods and men the father!
Who for Danae and Europa
Changed thy shape, thou bold eloper!

Hear me, god! ye gods all, hear me!
Such a sin came never near me.
Hear, thou god! and gods all, hear ye!
Thus I sinned not, as I fear ye.

I by Mars vow, by Apollo,
Both of whom Love's learning follow;
Yea, by Cupid too, the terror
Of whose bow forbids all error!

By thy bow I vow and quiver,
By the shafts thou dost deliver,
Without fraud, in honour duly
To observe my troth-plight truly.

I will keep the troth I plighted,
And the reason shall be cited :
'Tis that 'mid the girls no maiden
Ever met I more love-laden.

'Mid the girls thou art beholden
Like a pearl in setting golden ;
Yea, thy shoulder, neck, and bosom
Bear of beauty's self the blossom.

Oh, her throat, lips, forehead, nourish
Love, with food that makes him flourish !
And her curls, I did adore them—
They were blonde with heaven's light o'er them.

Therefore, till, for Nature's scorning,
Toil is rest and midnight morning,
Till no trees in woods are growing,
Till fire turns to water flowing ;

Till seas have no ships to sail them,
Till the Parthians' arrows fail them,
I, my girl, will love thee ever,
Unbetrayed, betray thee never !

In the following poem a lover bids adieu for ever to an unworthy woman, who has betrayed him. This is a remarkable specimen of the songs written for a complicated melody. The first eight lines seem set to one tune; in the next four that tune is slightly accelerated, and a double rhyme is substituted for a single one in the tenth and twelfth verses. The five concluding lines go to a different kind of melody, and express in each stanza a changed mood of feeling.

I have tried in this instance to adopt the plaster-cast method of translation, as described above,[1] and have even endeavoured to obtain the dragging effect of the first eight lines of each strophe, which are composed neither of exact accentual dactyls nor yet of exact accentual anapaests, but offer a good example of that laxity of rhythm permitted in this prosody for music.

Comparison with the original will show that I was not copying Byron's *When we Two Parted*; yet the resemblance between that song and the tone which my translation has naturally assumed from the Latin, is certainly noticeable. That Byron could have seen the piece before he wrote his own lines in question is almost impossible, for this portion of the *Carmina Burana* had not, so far as I am aware, been edited

[1] Page 46.

before the year 1847. The coincidence of metrical
form, so far as it extends, only establishes the spontaneity of emotion which, in the case of the medieval
and the modern poet, found a similar rhythm for the
utterance of similar feeling.

FAREWELL TO THE FAITHLESS

No. 40

A MORTAL anguish
    How often woundeth me:
Grieving I languish,
  Weighed down with misery;
Hearing the mournful
  Tale of thy fault and fall
Blown by Fame's scornful
  Trump to the ears of all!

Envious rumour
  Late or soon will slay thee:
Love with less humour,
  Lest thy love betray thee.

Whate'er thou dost, do secretly,
Far from Fame's curiosity;

Love in the dark delights to be,
His sports are wiles and witchery,
  With laugh of lovers greeting.

Thou wert not slighted,
  Stained in thine honour, when
We were united,
  Lovers unknown to men ;
But when thy passion
  Grew like thy bosom cold,
None had compassion,
  Then was thy story told.

Fame, who rejoiceth
  New amours to utter,
Now thy shame voiceth,
  Wide her pinions flutter.

The palace home of modesty
Is made a haunt for harlotry ;
The virgin lily you may see
Defiled by fingers lewd and free,
  With vile embraces meeting.

I mourn the tender
  Flower of the youth of thee,
Brighter in splendour
  Than evening's star can be.

Pure were thy kisses,
  Dove-like thy smile;
As the snake hisses
  Now is thy guile.

Lovers who pray thee
  From thy door are scattered;
Lovers who pay thee
  In thy bed are flattered.

Thou bidst them from thy presence flee
From whom thou canst not take thy fee;
Blind, halt, and lame thy suitors be;
Illustrious men with subtlety
  And poisonous honey cheating.

I may add that a long soliloquy printed in *Carmina Burana*, pp. 119–121, should be compared with the foregoing lyric. It has a similar motive, though the lover in this case expresses his willingness for reconciliation. One part of its expostulation with the faithless woman is beautiful in its simplicity :—

" Amaveram prae caeteris
  Te, sed amici veteris
  Es jam oblita!   Superis
  Vel inferis
  Ream te criminamur."

I will close this section with the lament written for a medieval Gretchen whose fault has been discovered, and whose lover has been forced to leave the country. Its bare realism contrasts with the lyrical exuberance of the preceding specimens.

GRETCHEN

No. 41

UP to this time, well-away!
　　I concealed the truth from day,
　Went on loving skilfully.
Now my fault at length is clear:
That the hour of need is near,
　From my shape all eyes can see.
So my mother gives me blows,
So my father curses throws;
　They both treat me savagely.
In the house alone I sit,
Dare not walk about the street,
　Nor at play in public be.

If I walk about the street,
Every one I chance to meet
　Scans me like a prodigy:

When they see the load I bear,
All the neighbours nudge and stare,
   Gaping while I hasten by;
With their elbows nudge, and so
With their finger point, as though
   I were some monstrosity;
Me with nods and winks they spurn,
Judge me fit in flames to burn
   For one lapse from honesty.

Why this tedious tale prolong?
Short, I am become a song,
   In all mouths a mockery.
By this am I done to death,
Sorrow kills me, chokes my breath,
   Ever weep I bitterly.
One thing makes me still more grieve,
That my friend his home must leave
   For the same cause instantly;
Therefore is my sadness so
Multiplied, weighed down with woe,
   For he too will part from me.

XVIII

A separate section should be assigned to poems of exile. They are not very numerous, but are interesting in connection with the wandering life of their vagrant authors. The first has all the dreamy pathos felt by a young German leaving his beloved home in some valley of the Suabian or Thuringian hills.

ADIEU TO THE VALLEY

No. 42

OH, of love twin-brother anguish!
  In thy pangs I faint and languish,
   Cannot find relief from thee!
Nay, no marvel! I must grieve her,
Wander forth in exile, leave her,
   Who hath gained the heart of me;
Who of loveliness so rare is
That for her sake Trojan Paris
   Would have left his Helenë.

Smile, thou valley, sweetest, fairest,
Wreathed with roses of the rarest,
   Flower of all the vales that be!

Vale of vales, all vales excelling,
Sun and moon thy praise are telling,
    With the song-birds' melody ;
Nightingales thy praise are singing,
O thou soothing solace-bringing
    To the soul's despondency !

The second was probably intended to be sung at a drinking-party by a student taking leave of his companions. It is love that forces him to quit their society and to break with his studies. The long rhyming lines, followed by a sharp drop at the close of each stanza upon a short disjointed phrase, seem to indicate discouragement and melancholy.

THE LOVER'S PARTING

No. 43

SWEET native soil, farewell ! dear country of
    my birth !
Fair chamber of the loves ! glad home of joy and
    mirth !
To-morrow or to-day I leave you, o'er the earth
To wander struck with love, to pine with rage and
    dearth
                                In exile !

Farewell, sweet land, and ye, my comrades dear,
 adieu !
To whom with kindly heart I have been ever true ;
The studies that we loved I may no more pursue ;
Weep then for me, who part as though I died to you,
   Love-laden !

As many as the flowers that Hybla's valley cover,
As many as the leaves that on Dodona hover,
As many as the fish that sail the wide seas over,
So many are the pangs that pain a faithful lover,
   For ever !

With the new fire of love my wounded bosom burns ;
Love knows not any ruth, all tender pity spurns ;
How true the proverb speaks that saith to him that
 yearns,
" Where love is there is pain ; thy pleasure love
 returns
   With anguish ! "

Ah, sorrow ! ah, how sad the wages of our bliss !
In lovers' hearts the flame's too hot for happiness ;
For Venus still doth send new sighs and new distress
When once the enamoured soul is taken with excess
   Of sweetness !

The third introduces us to a little episode of medieval private life which must have been frequent enough.
It consists of a debate between a father and his son
upon the question whether the young man should enter
into a monastic brotherhood.   The youth is lying on
a sickbed, and thinks that he is already at the point of
death.   It will be noticed that he is only diverted
from his project by the mention of a student friend
(indicated, as usual, by an N), whom he would never
be able to see again if he assumed the cowl.   I suspect,
however, that the poem has not been transmitted to
us entire.

IN ARTICULO MORTIS

No. 44

Son. OH, my father ! help, I pray !
       Death is near my soul to-day ;
With your blessing let me be
Made a monk right speedily !

See the foe my life invade !
Haste, oh haste, to give me aid !
Bring me comfort and heart's ease,
Strengthen me in this disease !

Father. Oh, my best-belovèd son,
      What is this thou wouldst have done?
      Weigh it well in heart and brain:
      Do not leave me here in pain.

Son. Father, this thy loving care
      Makes me weep full sore, I swear;
      For you will be childless when
      I have joined those holy men.

Father. Therefore make a little stay,
      Put it off till the third day;
      It may be your danger is
      Not unto the death, I wis.

Son. Such the anguish that I feel
      Through my inmost entrails steal,
      That I bide in doubt lest death
      Ere to-morrow end my breath.

Father. Those strict rules that monks observe,
      Well I know them! They must serve
      Heaven by fasting every day,
      And by keeping watch alway.

Son. Who for God watch through the night
      Shall receive a crown of light;
      Who for heaven's sake hungers, he
      Shall be fed abundantly.

Father. Hard and coarse the food they eat,
    Beans and pottage-herbs their meat;
    After such a banquet, think,
    Water is their only drink!

Son. What's the good of feasts, or bright
    Cups of Bacchus, when, in spite
    Of all comforts, at the last
    This poor flesh to worms is cast?

Father. Well, then, let thy parent's moan
    Move thee in thy soul, my son!
    Mourning for thee made a monk,
    Dead-alive in darkness sunk.

Son. They who father, mother love,
    And their God neglect, will prove
    That they are in error found
    When the judgment trump shall sound.

Father. Logic! would thou ne'er hadst been
    Known on earth for mortal teen!
    Many a clerk thou mak'st to roam
    Wretched, exiled from his home.—

    Never more thine eyes, my son,
    Shall behold thy darling one,
    Him, that little clerk so fair,
    N., thy friend beyond compare!

Son. Oh, alas! unhappy me!
     What to do I cannot see;
     Wandering lost in exile so,
     Without guide or light I go!—

     Dry your tears, my father dear,
     Haply there is better cheer;
     Now my mind on change is set,
     I'll not be a monk, not yet.

XIX

The order adopted in this essay brings us now to drinking-songs. Next to spring and love, our students set their affections principally on the tavern and the wine-bowl. In the poems on the Order we have seen how large a space in their vagrant lives was occupied by the tavern and its jovial company of topers and gamesters. It was there that—

    "Some are gaming, some are drinking,
    Some are living without thinking;
    And of those who make the racket,
    Some are stripped of coat and jacket;
    Some get clothes of finer feather,
    Some are cleaned out altogether;
    No one there dreads death's invasion,
    But all drink in emulation."

The song from which I have extracted this stanza contains a parody of S. Thomas Aquinas' hymn on the Eucharist.[1]   To translate it seemed to me impossible; but I will cite the following stanza, which may be compared with stanzas ix. and x. of *Lauda Sion* :—

> "Bibit hera, bibit herus,
> Bibit miles, bibit clerus,
> Bibit ille, bibit illa,
> Bibit servus cum ancilla,
> Bibit velox, bibit piger,
> Bibit albus, bibit niger,
> Bibit constans, bibit vagus,
> Bibit rudis, bibit magus."

Several of the best anacreontics of the period are even more distinctly parodies.   The following panegyric of wine, for example, is modelled upon a hymn to the Virgin :—

A SEQUENCE IN PRAISE OF WINE

No. 45

WINE the good and bland, thou blessing
   Of the good, the bad's distressing,
Sweet of taste by all confessing,
   Hail, thou world's felicity !

[1] *In Taberna, Carm. Bur.*, p. 235.

Hail thy hue, life's gloom dispelling;
Hail thy taste, all tastes excelling;
By thy power, in this thy dwelling
   Deign to make us drunk with thee!

Oh, how blest for bounteous uses
Is the birth of pure vine-juices!
Safe's the table which produces
   Wine in goodly quality.
Oh, in colour how auspicious!
Oh, in odour how delicious!
In the mouth how sweet, propitious
   To the tongue enthralled by thee!

Blest the man who first thee planted,
Called thee by thy name enchanted!
He whose cups have ne'er been scanted
   Dreads no danger that may be.
Blest the belly where thou bidest!
Blest the tongue where thou residest!
Blest the mouth through which thou glidest,
   And the lips thrice blest by thee!

Therefore let wine's praise be sounded,
Healths to topers all propounded;
We shall never be confounded,
   Toping for eternity!

Pray we : here be thou still flowing,
Plenty on our board bestowing,
While with jocund voice we're showing
   How we serve thee—Jubilee !

Another, regarding the date of which I have no
information, is an imitation of a well-known *Christmas
Carol.*

A CAROL OF WINE

No. 46

IN dulci jubilo
   Sing we, make merry so !
   Since our heart's pleasure
Latet in poculo,
   Drawn from the cask, good measure,
Pro hoc convivio,
      Nunc, nunc bibito !

O crater parvule !
Hòw my soul yearns for thee !
   Make me now merry,
O potus optime,
   Claret or hock or sherry !
Et vos concinite :
      Vivant socii !

O vini caritas !
O Bacchi lenitas !
  We've drained our purses
Per multa pocula :
  Yet hope we for new mercies,
Nummorum gaudia :
    Would that we had them, ah.

Ubi sunt gaudia ? where,
If that they be not there ?
  There the lads are singing
Selecta cantica :
  There are glasses ringing
In villae curia ;
    Oh, would that we were there !

In Dulci Jubilo yields an example of mixed Latin and German. This is the case too with a comparatively ancient drinking-song quoted by Geiger in his *Renaissance und Humanismus*, p. 414. It may be mentioned that the word *Bursae*, for *Burschen*, occurs in stanza v. This word, to indicate a student, can also be found in *Carm. Bur.*, p. 236, where we are introduced to scholars drinking yellow Rhine wine out of glasses of a pale pink colour—already in the twelfth century !

THE STUDENTS' WINE-BOUT

No. 47

HO, all ye jovial brotherhood,
　　Quos sitis vexat plurima,
I know a host whose wits are good,
　　Quod vina spectat optima.

His wine he blends not with the juice
　　E puteo qui sumitur;
Each kind its virtue doth produce
　　E botris ut exprimitur.

Host, bring us forth good wine and strong,
　　In cella quod est optimum!
We brethren will our sport prolong
　　Ad noctis usque terminum.

Whoso to snarl or bite is fain,
　　Ut canes decet rabidos,
Outside our circle may remain,
　　Ad porcos eat sordidos.

Hurrah! my lads, we'll merry make!
　　Levate sursum pocula!
God's blessing on all wine we take,
　　In sempiterna saecula!

Two lyrics of distinguished excellence, which still
hold their place in the *Commersbuch*, cannot claim
certain antiquity in their present form. They are not
included in the *Carmina Burana;* yet their style is so
characteristic of the Archipoeta, that I believe we may
credit him with at least a share in their composition.
The first starts with an allusion to the Horatian *tempus
edax rerum.*

TIME'S A-FLYING

No. 48

LAUREL-CROWNED Horatius,
   True, how true thy saying!
Swift as wind flies over us
   Time, devouring, slaying.
Where are, oh! those goblets full
   Of wine honey-laden,
Strifes and loves and bountiful
   Lips of ruddy maiden?

Grows the young grape tenderly,
   And the maid is growing;
But the thirsty poet, see,
   Years on him are snowing!

What's the use on hoary curls
Of the bays undying,
If we may not kiss the girls,
Drink while time's a-flying?

The second consists of a truly brilliant development
of the theme which our Herrick condensed into one
splendid phrase—"There's no lust like to poetry!"

THERE'S NO LUST LIKE TO POETRY

No. 49

SWEET in goodly fellowship
Tastes red wine and rare O!
But to kiss a girl's ripe lip
Is a gift more fair O!
Yet a gift more sweet, more fine,
Is the lyre of Maro!
While these three good gifts were mine,
I'd not change with Pharaoh.

Bacchus wakes within my breast
Love and love's desire,
Venus comes and stirs the blessed
Rage of Phœbus' fire;

Deathless honour is our due
From the laurelled sire :
Woe should I turn traitor to
Wine and love and lyre !

Should a tyrant rise and say,
"Give up wine !" I'd do it ;
"Love no girls !" I would obey,
Though my heart should rue it.
"Dash thy lyre !" suppose he saith,
Naught should bring me to it ;
"Yield thy lyre or die !" my breath,
Dying, should thrill through it !

A lyric of the elder period in praise of wine and love, which forcibly illustrates the contempt felt by the student class for the unlettered laity and boors, shall be inserted here. It seems to demand a tune.

WINE AND VENUS

No. 50

HO, comrades mine !
What is your pleasure ?
What business fine
Or mirthful measure ?

Lo, Venus toward our crew advancing,
A choir of Dryads round her dancing!

Good fellows you!
The time is jolly!
Earth springs anew,
Bans melancholy;
Bid long farewell to winter weather!
Let lads and maids be blithe together.

Dame Venus spurns
Her brother Ocean;
To Bacchus turns;
No colder potion
Deserves her godhead's approbation;
On sober souls she pours damnation.

Let then this band,
Imbued with learning,
By Venus stand,
Her wages earning!
Laymen we spurn from our alliance,
Like brutes to art deaf, dumb to science.

Two gods alone
We serve and mate with;
One law we own,
Nor hold debate with:

Who lives the goodly student fashion
Must love and win love back with passion!

Among drinking-songs of the best period in this
literature may be reckoned two disputations between
water and wine. In the one, Thetis defends herself
against Lyaeus, and the poet assists in vision at their
contest. The scene is appropriately laid in the third
sphere, the pleasant heaven of Venus. The other,
which on the whole appears to me preferable, and
which I have therefore chosen for translation, begins
and ends with the sound axiom that water and wine
ought never to be mixed. It is manifest that the poet
reserves the honour of the day for wine, though his
arguments are fair to both sides. The final point,
which breaks the case of water down and determines
her utter confusion, is curious, since it shows that
people in the Middle Ages were fully alive to the
perils of sewage-contaminated wells.

THE CONTEST OF WINE AND WATER

No. 51

LAYING truth bare, stripped of fable,
Briefly as I may be able,
With good reasons manifold,

I will tell why man should never
Copulate, but rather sever,
   Things that strife and hatred hold.

When one cup in fell confusion
Wine with water blends, the fusion,
   Call it by what name you will,
Is no blessing, nor deserveth
Any praise, but rather serveth
   For the emblem of all ill.

Wine perceives the water present,
And with pain exclaims, " What peasant
   Dared to mingle thee with me ?
Rise, go forth, get out, and leave me !
In the same place, here to grieve me,
   Thou hast no just claim to be.

" Vile and shameless in thy going,
Into cracks thou still art flowing,
   That in foul holes thou mayst lie ;
O'er the earth thou ought'st to wander,
On the earth thy liquor squander,
   And at length in anguish die.

" How canst thou adorn a table ?
No one sings or tells a fable
   In thy presence dull and drear ;

But the guest who erst was jolly,
Laughing, joking, bent on folly,
　　Silent sits when thou art near.

"Should one drink of thee to fulness,
Sound before, he takes an illness;
　　All his bowels thou dost stir;
Booms the belly, wind ariseth,
Which, enclosed and pent, surpriseth
　　With a thousand sighs the ear.

"When the stomach's so inflated,
Blasts are then ejaculated
　　From both draughts with divers sound;
And that organ thus affected,
All the air is soon infected
　　By the poison breathed around."

Water thus wine's home-thrust warded:
"All thy life is foul and sordid,
　　Sunk in misery, steeped in vice;
Those who drink thee lose their morals,
Waste their time in sloth and quarrels,
　　Rolling down sin's precipice.

"Thou dost teach man's tongue to stutter;
He goes reeling in the gutter
　　Who hath deigned to kiss thy lips;

Hears men speak without discerning,
Sees a hundred tapers burning
   When there are but two poor dips.

"He who feels for thee soul's hunger
Is a murderer or whoremonger,
   Davus Geta Birria;
Such are they whom thou dost nourish;
With thy fame and name they flourish
   In the tavern's disarray.

"Thou by reason of thy badness
Art confined in prison sadness,
   Cramped and small thy dwellings are:
I am great the whole world over,
Spread myself abroad and cover
   Every part of earth afar.

"Drink I yield to palates burning;
They who for soul's health are yearning,
   Need the aid that I have given;
Since all pilgrims, at their praying,
Far or near, I am conveying
   To the palaces of heaven."

Wine replied: "What thou hast vaunted
Proves thee full of fraud; for granted
   That thou carriest ships o'er sea,

Yet thou then dost swell and riot;
Till they wreck thou hast no quiet;
 Thus they are deceived through thee.

" He whose strength is insufficient
Thee to slake with heat efficient,
 Sunk in mortal peril lies :
Trusting thee the poor wretch waneth,
And through thee at length attaineth
 To the joys of Paradise.

" I'm a god, as that true poet
Naso testifies; men owe it
 Unto me that they are sage;
When they do not drink, professors
Lose their wits and lack assessors
 Round about the lecture-stage.

" 'Tis impossible to sever
Truth from falsehood if you never
 Learn to drink my juices neat.
Thanks to me, dumb speak, deaf listen,
Blind folk see, the senses glisten,
 And the lame man finds his feet.

" Eld through me to youth returneth,
While thine influence o'erturneth
 All a young man's lustihead;

By my force the world is laden
With new births, but boy or maiden
   Through thy help was never bred."

Water saith : "A god thou !   Just men
By thy craft become unjust men,
   Bad, worse, worst, degenerous !
Thanks to thee, their words half uttered
Through the drunken lips are stuttered,
   And thy sage is Didymus.

" I will speak the truth out wholly :
Earth bears fruit by my gift solely,
   And the meadows bloom in May ;
When it rains not, herbs and grasses
Dry with drought, spring's beauty passes,
   Flowers and lilies fade away.

" Lo, thy crookèd mother pining,
On her boughs the grapes declining,
   Barren through the dearth of rain ;
Mark her tendrils lean and sterile
O'er the parched earth at their peril
   Bent in unavailing pain !

" Famine through all lands prevaileth,
Terror-struck the people waileth,
   When I choose to keep away ;

Christians kneel to Christ to gain me,
Jews and Pagans to obtain me
 Ceaseless vows and offerings pay."

Wine saith : " To the deaf thou'rt singing,
Those vain self-laudations flinging !
 Otherwhere thou hast been shown !
Patent 'tis to all the races
How impure and foul thy place is ;
 We believe what we have known !

" Thou of things the scum and rotten
Sewer, where ordures best forgotten
 And unmentioned still descend !
Filth and garbage, stench and poison,
Thou dost bear in fetid foison !
 Here I stop lest words offend."

Water rose, the foe invaded,
In her own defence upbraided
 Wine for his invective base :
" Now at last we've drawn the curtain !
Who, what god thou art is certain
 From thy oracle's disgrace.

" This thine impudent oration
Hurts not me ; 'tis desecration
 To a god, and fouls his tongue !

At the utmost at nine paces
Can I suffer filthy places,
    Fling far from me dirt and dung ! "

Wine saith : " This repudiation
Of my well-weighed imputation
    Doth not clear thyself of crime !
Many a man and oft who swallowed
Thine infected potion, followed
    After death in one day's time."

Hearing this, in stupefaction
Water stood ; no words, no action,
    Now restrained her sobs of woe.
Wine exclaims, " Why art thou dumb then?
Without answer ?   Is it come then
    To thy complete overthrow ? "

I who heard the whole contention
Now declare my song's intention,
    And to all the world proclaim :
They who mix these things shall ever
Henceforth be accursed, and never
    In Christ's kingdom portion claim.

The same precept, " Keep wine and water apart,"
is conveyed at the close of a lyric distinguished in

other respects for the brutal passion of its drunken
fervour.   I have not succeeded in catching the rollick-
ing swing of the original verse ; and I may observe
that the last two stanzas seem to form a separate song,
although their metre is the same as that of the first
four.

BACCHIC FRENZY

No. 52

TOPERS in and out of season!
   'Tis not thirst but better reason
Bids you tope on steadily !—
Pass the wine-cup, let it be
Filled and filled for bout on bout !
     Never sleep !
Racy jest and song flash out !
     Spirits leap !

Those who cannot drink their rations,
Go, begone from these ovations !
   Here's no place for bashful boys ;
   Like the plague, they spoil our joys.—
Bashful eyes bring rustic cheer
     When we're drunk,
And a blush betrays a drear
     Want of spunk.

If there's here a fellow lurking
Who his proper share is shirking,
    Let the door to him be shown,
    From our crew we'll have him thrown ;—
He's more desolate than death,
            Mixed with us ;
    Let him go and end his breath !
            Better thus !

When your heart is set on drinking,
Drink on without stay or thinking,
    Till you cannot stand up straight,
    Nor one word articulate !—
But herewith I pledge to you
            This fair health :
    May the glass no mischief do,
            Bring you wealth !

Wed not you the god and goddess,
For the god doth scorn the goddess ;
    He whose name is Liber, he
    Glories in his liberty.
    All her virtue in the cup
            Runs to waste,
    And wine wedded yieldeth up
            Strength and taste.

Since she is the queen of ocean,
Goddess she may claim devotion:
    But she is no mate to kiss
    His superior holiness.
Bacchus never deigned to be
        Watered, he !
Liber never bore to be
        Christened, he !

XX

Closely allied to drinking-songs are some comic ditties which may have been sung at wine-parties. Of these I have thought it worth while to present a few specimens, though their medieval bluntness of humour does not render them particularly entertaining to a modern reader.

The first I have chosen is *The Lament of the Roast Swan*. It must be remembered that this bird was esteemed a delicacy in the Middle Ages, and also that pepper was highly prized for its rarity. This gives a certain point to the allusion in the third stanza.

THE LAMENT OF THE ROAST SWAN

No. 53

TIME was my wings were my delight,
Time was I made a lovely sight;
'Twas when I was a swan snow-white.
Woe's me! I vow,
Black am I now,
Burned up, back, beak, and brow!

The baster turns me on the spit,
The fire I've felt the force of it,
The carver carves me bit by bit.

I'd rather in the water float
Under the bare heavens like a boat,
Than have this pepper down my throat.

Whiter I was than wool or snow,
Fairer than any bird I know;
Now am I blacker than a crow.

Now in the gravy-dish I lie,
I cannot swim, I cannot fly,
Nothing but gnashing teeth I spy.
Woe's me! I vow, &c.

The next is *The Last Will of the Dying Ass.* There
is not much to be said for the wit of this piece.

THE WILL OF THE DYING ASS

No. 54

WHILE a boor, as poets tell,
  Whacked his patient ass too well,
On the ground half dead it fell.
      La sol fa,
On the ground half dead it fell,
      La sol fa mi re ut.

Then with gesture sad and low,
Streaming eyes and words of woe,
He at length addressed it so :

" Had I known, my gentle ass,
Thou from me so soon wouldst pass,
I'd have swaddled thee, alas !

" Made for thee a tunic meet,
Shirt and undershirt complete,
Breeches, drawers of linen sweet.

" Rise awhile, for pity's sake,
That ere life your limbs forsake
You your legacies may make ! "

Soon the ass stood up, and thus,
With a weak voice dolorous,
His last will proclaimed for us :

" To the magistrates my head,
Eyes to constables," he said,
" Ears to judges, when I'm dead ;

" To old men my teeth shall fall,
Lips to wanton wooers all,
And my tongue to wives that brawl.

" Let my feet the bailiffs win,
Nostrils the tobacco-men,
And fat canons take my skin.

" Voice to singing boys I give,
Throat to topers, may they live !
**** to students amative.

*** on shepherds I bestow,
Thistles on divines, and lo !
To the law my shade shall go.

" Elders have my tardy pace,
Boys my rude and rustic grace,
Monks my simple open face."

He who saith this testament
Will not hold, let him be shent;
He's an ass by all consent.
La sol fa,
He's an ass by all consent,
La sol fa mi re ut.

As a third specimen I select a little bit of mixed
prose and verse from the *Carmina Burana*, which is
curious from its allusion to the Land of Cockaigne.
Goliardic literature, it may be parenthetically observed,
has some strong pieces of prose comedy and satire.
Of these, the *Mass of Topers* and *Mass of Gamesters*,
the *Gospel according to Marks*, and the description of a
fat monk's daily life deserve quotation.[1] They are
for the most part, however, too profane to bear
translation.

THE ABBOT OF COCKAIGNE

No. 55

I AM the Abbot of Cockaigne,
And this is my counsel with topers;
And in the sect of Decius (gamesters) this is my will;

[1] Wright's *Rel. Ant.*, ii.; *Carm. Bur.*, pp. 248 and 22;
Wright's *Mapes*, p. xl.

And whoso shall seek me in taverns before noon ;
After evensong shall he go forth naked,
And thus, stripped of raiment, shall lament him :
    Wafna ! wafna !
   O Fate most foul, what hast thou done ?
   The joys of man beneath the sun
   Thou hast stolen, every one !

XXI

The transition from these trivial and slightly interesting comic songs to poems of a serious import, which played so important a part in Goliardic literature, must of necessity be abrupt. It forms no part of my present purpose to exhibit the Wandering Students in their capacity as satirists. That belongs more properly to a study of the earlier Reformation than to such an inquiry as I have undertaken in this treatise. Satires, especially medieval satires, are apt, besides, to lose their force and value in translation. I have therefore confined myself to five specimens, more or less closely connected with the subjects handled in this study.

The first has the interest of containing some ideas which Villon preserved in his ballad of the men of old time.

DEATH TAKES ALL

No. 56

HEAR, O thou earth, hear, thou encircling sea,
　　Yea, all that live beneath the sun, hear ye
How of this world the bravery and the glory
Are but vain forms and shadows transitory,
Even as all things 'neath Time's empire show
By their short durance and swift overthrow !

　Nothing avails the dignity of kings,
Naught, naught avail the strength and stuff of things,
The wisdom of the arts no succour brings ;
Genus and species help not at death's hour,
No man was saved by gold in that dread stour ;
The substance of things fadeth as a flower,
As ice 'neath sunshine melts into a shower.

　Where is Plato, where is Porphyrius ?
Where is Tullius, where is Virgilius ?
Where is Thales, where is Empedocles,
Or illustrious Aristoteles ?
Where's Alexander, peerless of might ?
Where is Hector, Troy's stoutest knight ?
Where is King David, learning's light ?
Solomon where, that wisest wight ?

Where is Helen, and Paris rose-bright?
    They have fallen to the bottom, as a stone rolls:
Who knows if rest be granted to their souls?
    But Thou, O God, of faithful men the Lord,
To us Thy favour evermore afford
When on the wicked judgment shall be poured!

The second marks the passage from those feelings
of youth and springtime which have been copiously
illustrated in Sections xiv.–xvii., to emotions befitting
later manhood and life's autumn.

AUTUMN YEARS

No. 57

WHILE life's April blossom blew,
    What I willed I then might do,
Lust and law seemed comrades true.
        As I listed, unresisted,
Hither, thither, could I play,
And my wanton flesh obey.

When life's autumn days decline,
Thus to live, a libertine,
Fancy-free as thoughts incline,
        Manhood's older age and colder

Now forbids; removes, destroys
All those ways of wonted joys.

Age with admonition wise
Thus doth counsel and advise,
While her voice within me cries:
      " For repenting and relenting
There is room; forgiveness falls
On all contrite prodigals! "

I will seek a better mind;
Change, correct, and leave behind
What I did with purpose blind:
      From vice sever, with endeavour
Yield my soul to serious things,
Seek the joy that virtue brings.

The third would find a more appropriate place in a
hymn-book than in a collection of *Carmina Vagorum.*
It is, however, written in a lyrical style so closely
allied to the secular songs of the *Carmina Burana*
(where it occurs) that I have thought it well to quote
its grimly medieval condemnation of human life.

VANITAS VANITATUM

No. 58

THIS vile world
  In madness hurled
    Offers but false shadows;
Joys that wane
And waste like vain
    Lilies of the meadows.

Worldly wealth,
Youth, strength, and health,
    Cramp the soul's endeavour;
Drive it down
In hell to drown,
    Hell that burns for ever.

What we see,
And what let be,
    While on earth we tarry,
We shall cast
Like leaves at last
    Which the sere oaks carry

Carnal life,
Man's law of strife,

Hath but brief existence;
Passes, fades,
Like wavering shades
 Without real subsistence.

Therefore bind,
Tread down and grind
 Fleshly lusts that blight us;
So heaven's bliss
'Mid saints that kiss
 Shall for aye delight us.

The fourth, in like manner, would have but little
to do with a Commersbuch, were it not for the fact
that the most widely famous modern student-song of
Germany has borrowed two passages from its serious
and tragic rhythm. Close inspection of *Gaudeamus
Igitur* shows that the metrical structure of that song is
based on the principle of quoting one of its long lines
and rhyming to it.

ON CONTEMPT FOR THE WORLD

No. 59

"DE contemptu mundi:" this is the theme I've
taken:
Time it is from sleep to rise, from death's torpor
waken:
Gather virtue's grain and leave tares of sin forsaken.
Rise up, rise, be vigilant; trim your lamp, be
ready.

Brief is life, and brevity briefly shall be ended:
Death comes quick, fears no man, none hath his dart
suspended:
Death kills all, to no man's prayer hath he con-
descended.
Rise up, rise, be vigilant; trim your lamp, be
ready.

Where are they who in this world, ere we kept, were
keeping?
Come unto the churchyard, thou! see where they are
sleeping!

Dust and ashes are they, worms in their flesh are
    creeping.
    Rise up, rise, be vigilant; trim your lamp, be
    ready.

Into life each man is born with great teen and trouble:
All through life he drags along; toil on toil is double:
When life's done, the pangs of death take him, break
    the bubble.
    Rise up, rise, be vigilant; trim your lamp, be
    ready.

If from sin thou hast been turned, born a new man
    wholly,
Changed thy life to better things, childlike, simple,
    holy;
Thus into God's realm shalt thou enter with the
    lowly.
    Rise up, rise, be vigilant; trim your lamp, be
    ready.

Having alluded to *Gaudeamus Igitur*, I shall close
my translations with a version of it into English. The
dependence of this lyric upon the rhythm and substance
of the poem on *Contempt for the World*, which I have
already indicated, is perhaps the reason why it is sung
by German students after the funeral of a comrade.

The Office for the Dead sounding in their ears, occasions the startling *igitur* with which it opens; and their mind reverts to solemn phrases in the midst of masculine determination to enjoy the present while it is yet theirs.

GAUDEAMUS IGITUR

No. 60

L ET us live, then, and be glad
    While young life's before us!
        After youthful pastime had,
        After old age hard and sad,
    Earth will slumber o'er us.

Where are they who in this world,
    Ere we kept, were keeping?
        Go ye to the gods above;
        Go to hell; inquire thereof:
    They are not; they're sleeping.

Brief is life, and brevity
    Briefly shall be ended:
        Death comes like a whirlwind strong,
        Bears us with his blast along;
    None shall be defended.

Live this university,
  Men that learning nourish ;
      Live each member of the same,
      Long live all that bear its name ;
  Let them ever flourish !

Live the commonwealth also,
  And the men that guide it !
      Live our town in strength and health,
      Founders, patrons, by whose wealth
  We are here provided !

Live all girls ! A health to you,
  Melting maids and beauteous !
      Live the wives and women too,
      Gentle, loving, tender, true,
  Good, industrious, duteous !

Perish cares that pule and pine !
  Perish envious blamers !
      Die the Devil, thine and mine !
      Die the starch-necked Philistine !
  Scoffers and defamers !

XXII

I have now fulfilled the purpose which I had in view when I began this study of the *Carmina Vagorum*, and have reproduced in English verse what seemed to me the most characteristic specimens of that literature, in so far as it may be considered precursory of the Renaissance.

In spite of novelty, in spite of historical interest, in spite of a certain literary charm, it is not an edifying product of medieval art with which I have been dealing. When I look back upon my own work, and formulate the impression left upon my mind by familiarity with the songs I have translated, the doubt occurs whether some apology be not required for having dragged these forth from antiquarian obscurity.

The truth is that there is very little that is elevated in the lyrics of the Goliardi. They are almost wholly destitute of domestic piety, of patriotism, of virtuous impulse, of heroic resolve. The greatness of an epoch which throbbed with the enthusiasms of the Crusades, which gave birth to a Francis and a Dominic, which witnessed the manly resistance offered by the Lombard burghs to the Teutonic Emperor, the formation of

Northern France into a solid monarchy, and the victorious struggle of the Papacy against the Empire, finds but rare expression in this poetry. From the *Carmina Burana* we cull one chant indeed on Saladin, one spirited lament for Richard Cœur de Lion; but their general tone is egotistic.

Even the satires, so remarkable for boldness, are directed against those ecclesiastical abuses which touched the interests of the clerkly classes—against simony, avarice, venality in the Roman Curia, against the ambition of prelates and the effort to make princely benefices hereditary, rather than against the real sins of the Church—her wilful solidification of popular superstitions for the purposes of self-aggrandisement, her cruel persecution of free thought, and her deflection from the spirit of her Founder.

With regard to women, abundant examples have been adduced to illustrate the sensual and unromantic spirit of these lettered lovers. A note of undisguised materialism sounds throughout the large majority of their erotic songs. Tenderness of feeling is rarely present. The passion is one-sided, recognised as ephemeral, without a vista on the sanctities of life in common with the beloved object. Notable exceptions to the general rule are the lyrics I have printed above on pp. 89-93. But it would have been easier to confirm the impression of licentiousness than to multiply specimens of delicate sentiment, had I chosen to ransack the whole stores of the *Carmina Burana.*

It is not necessary to censure their lack of so-called chivalrous woman-worship. That artificial mood of emotion, though glorified by the literary art of greatest poets, has something pitiably unreal, incurably morbid, in its mysticism. But, putting this aside, we are still bound to notice the absence of that far more human self-devotion of man to woman which forms a conspicuous element in the Arthurian romances. The love of Tristram for Iseult, of Lancelot for Guinevere, of Beaumains for his lady, is alien to the Goliardic conception of intersexual relations. Nowhere do we find a trace of Arthur's vow imposed upon his knights: "never to do outrage, . . . and alway to do ladies, damosels, and gentlewomen succour upon pain of death." This manly respect for women, which was, if not precisely the purest, yet certainly the most fruitful social impulse of the Middle Ages, receives no expression in the *Carmina Vagorum.*

The reason is not far to seek. The Clerici were a class debarred from domesticity, devoted in theory to celibacy, in practice incapable of marriage. They were not so much unsocial or anti-social as extra-social ; and while they gave a loose rein to their appetites, they respected none of those ties, anticipated none of those home pleasures, which consecrate the animal desires in everyday existence as we know it. One of their most popular poems is a brutal monastic diatribe on matrimony, fouler in its stupid abuse of women, more unmanly in its sordid imputations, than any satire which emanated from the corruption of Imperial Rome.[1] The cynicism of this exhortation against marriage forms a proper supplement to the other kind of cynicism which emerges in the lyrics of triumphant seducers and light lovers.

But why then have I taken the trouble to translate these songs, and to present them in such profusion to a modern audience ? It is because, after making all allowances for their want of great or noble feeling, due to the peculiar medium from which they sprang, they are in many ways realistically beautiful and in a strict sense true to vulgar human nature. They are the spontaneous expression of careless, wanton, unreflective youth. And all this they were, too, in an age which we are apt to regard as incapable of these very qualities.

The defects I have been at pains to indicate render the Goliardic poems remarkable as documents for the

[1] *Golias de Conjuge non ducenda*, Wright's *Mapes*, p. 77.

right understanding of the brilliant Renaissance epoch which was destined to close the Middle Ages. To the best of them we may with certainty assign the seventy-five years between 1150 and 1225. In that period, so fruitful of great efforts and of great results in the fields of politics and thought and literature, efforts and results foredoomed to partial frustration and to perverse mis-application—in that potent space of time, so varied in its intellectual and social manifestations, so pregnant with good and evil, so rapid in mutations, so inde-terminate between advance and retrogression—this Goliardic poetry stands alone. It occupies a position of unique and isolated, if limited, interest; because it was no outcome of feudalism or ecclesiasticism; because it has no tincture of chivalrous or mystic piety; because it implies no metaphysical determination; because it is pagan in the sense of being natural; because it is devoid of allegory, and, finally, because it is emphatically humanistic.

In these respects it detaches itself from the artistic and literary phenomena of the century which gave it birth. In these respects it anticipates the real eventual Renaissance.

There are, indeed, points of contact between the Stu-dents' Songs and other products of the Middle Ages. Scholastic quibblings upon words; reiterated commonplaces about spring; the brutal contempt for villeins; the frequent employment of hymn-rhythms and pre-occupation with liturgical phrases—these show that the Wandering Scholars were creatures of their age. But the qualities which this lyrical literature shares with that of the court, the temple, or the schools are mainly superficial; whereas the vital inspiration, the specific flavour, which render it noteworthy, are distinct and self-evolved. It is a premature, an unconscious effort made by a limited class to achieve *per saltum* what was slowly and laboriously wrought out by whole nations in the fifteenth and sixteenth centuries. Too precocious, too complete within too narrow limits, it was doomed to sterility. Not the least singular fact about it is that though the *Carmina Vagorum* continued to be appreciated, they were neither imitated nor developed to any definite extent after the period which I have indicated. They fell still-born upon the unreceptive soil of European culture at that epoch. Yet they fore-shadowed the mental and moral attitude which Europe was destined to assume when Italy through humanism gave its tone to the Renaissance.

The Renaissance, in Italy as elsewhere, had far more serious aims and enthusiasms in the direction of science, refined self-culture, discoveries, analysis of man and nature, than have always been ascribed to it. The men of that epoch did more hard work for the world, conferred more sterling benefits on their posterity, than those who study it chiefly from the point of view of art are ready to admit. But the mental atmosphere in which those heroes lived and wrought was one of carelessness with regard to moral duties and religious aspirations, of exuberant delight in pleasure as an object of existence. The glorification of the body and the senses, the repudiation of an ascetic tyranny which had long in theory imposed impossible abstentions on the carnal man, was a marked feature in their conception of the world; and connected with this was a return in no merely superficial spirit to the antique paganism of Greece and Rome.

These characteristics of the Renaissance we find already outlined with surprising definiteness, and at the same time with an almost childlike naïveté, a careless, mirth-provoking nonchalance, in the *Carmina Vagorum*. They remind us of the Italian lyrics which Lorenzo de' Medici and Poliziano wrote for the Florentine populace; and though in form and artistic intention they differ from the Latin verse of that period, their view of life is not dissimilar to that of a Pontano or a Beccadelli.

Some folk may regard the things I have presented to their view as ugly or insignificant, because they lack the higher qualities of sentiment; others may over-value them for precisely the same reason. They seem to me noteworthy as the first unmistakable sign of a change in modern Europe which was inevitable and predestined, as the first literary effort to restore the moral attitude of antiquity which had been displaced by medieval Christianity. I also feel the special relation which they bear to English poetry of the Elizabethan age— a relation that has facilitated their conversion into our language.

That Wandering Students of the twelfth century should have transcended the limitations of their age; that they should have absorbed so many elements of life into their scheme of natural enjoyment as the artists and scholars of the fifteenth; that they should have theorised their appetites and impulses with Valla, have produced masterpieces of poetry to rival Ariosto's, or criticisms of society in the style of Rabelais, was not to be expected. What their lyrics prove by anticipation is the sincerity of the so-called paganism of the Renaissance. When we read them, we perceive that that quality was substantially independent of the classical revival; though the influences of antique literature were eagerly seized upon as useful means for strengthening and giving tone to an already potent revolt of nature against hypocritical and palsy-stricken forms of spiritual despotism.

APPENDIX

See Section vii. pp. 19–27, above.

IT seems desirable that I should enlarge upon some topics which I treated somewhat summarily in Section vii. I assumed that the Wandering Scholars regarded themselves as a kind of Guild or Order; and for this assumption the Songs Nos. 1, 2, 3, translated in Section xiii. are a suffic. nt warrant. Yet the case might be considerably strengthened. In the *Sequentia falsi evangelii secundum marcam argenti*[1] we read of the *Gens Lusorum* or Tribe of Gamesters, which corresponds to the *Secta Decii*,[2] the *Ordo Vagorum*, and the *Familia Goliae*. Again, in Wright's *Walter Mapes*[3] there is an epistle written from England by one Richardus Goliardus to *Omnibus in Gallia Goliae discipulis*, introducing a friend, asking for information *ordo vester qualis*

[1] Grimm's *Gedichte des Mittelalters*, p. 232.
[2] *Carm. Bur.*, p. 254.   [3] Page 69.

est, and giving for the reason of this request *ne magis in ordine indiscrete vivam.* He addresses his French comrades as *pueri Goliae,* and winds up with good wishes for the *socios sanctae confratriae.* Proofs might be multiplied that the Wandering Students in Germany also regarded themselves as a confraternity, with special rules and ordinances. Of this, the curious parody of an episcopal letter, issued in 1209 by *Surianus, Praesul et Archiprimas,* to the *vagi clerici* of Austria, Styria, Bavaria, and Moravia is a notable example.[1]

I have treated Golias as the eponymous hero of this tribe, the chief of this confraternity. But it ought to be said that the name Golias occurs principally in English MSS., where the Goliardic poems are ascribed to *Golias Episcopus.* Elsewhere the same personage is spoken of as *Primas,* which is a title of dignity applying to a prelate with jurisdiction superior even to that of an archbishop. Grimm [2] quotes this phrase from a German chronicle : *Primas vagus multos versus edidit magistrales.* In the *Sequentia falsi evangelii* [3] we find twice repeated *Primas autem qui dicitur vilissimus.* The Venetian codex from which Grimm drew some of his texts [4]

---

[1] Giesebrecht in *Allg. Monatschrift,* Jan. 1853, p. 35.
[2] Op. cit., p. 182.   [3] Ibid., p. 232.
[4] Ibid., pp. 238, 239.

attributes the *Dispute of Thetis and Lyaeus* and the *Advice against Matrimony*, both of which passed in England under the name of Golias and afterwards of Walter Map, to *Primas Presbyter*.

With regard to this Primas, it is important to mention that Fra Salimbene in his Chronicle [1] gives a succinct account of him under the date 1233. It runs as follows: *Fuit his temporibus Primas canonicus coloniensis, magnus trutannus et magnus trufator, et maximus versificator et velox, qui, si dedisset cor suum ad diligendum Deum, magnus in litteratura divina fuisset, et utilis valde Ecclesiae Dei. Cujus Apocalypsim, quam fecerat, vidi, et alia scripta plura.* After this passage follow some anecdotes, with quotations of verses extemporised by Primas, and lastly the whole of the Confession, translated by me at p. 65 above. Thus Salimbene, who was almost a contemporary author, attributes to Primas two of the most important poems which passed in England under the name of Golias, while the Venetian MS. ascribes two others of the same class to Primas Presbyter. It is also very noteworthy that Salimbene expressly calls this Primas a Canon of Cologne.

That this poet, whoever he was, had attained to celebrity in Italy (as well as in Germany) under the

[1] Published at Parma, 1857.

title of Primas, appears also from the following passage of a treatise by Thomas of Capua [1] on the Art of Writing : *Dictaminum vero tria sunt genera auctoribus diffinita, prosaicum scilicet, metricum et rithmicum ; prosaicum ut Cassiodori, metricum ut Virgilii, rithmicum ut Primatis.* Boccaccio was in all probability referring to the same Primas in the tale he told about *Primasso,* [2] who is described as a man of European reputation, and a great and rapid versifier. It is curious that just as Giraldus seems to have accepted *Golias* as the real name of this poet, [3] so Fra Salimbene, Thomas of Capua, and Boccaccio appear to use *Primas* as a Christian name.

The matter becomes still more complicated when we find, as we do, some of the same poems attributed in France to Walter of Lille, in England to Walter Map, and further current under yet another title of dignity, that of *Archipoeta.* [4]

We can hardly avoid the conclusion that by Golias Episcopus, Primas, and Archipoeta one and the same person, occupying a prominent post in the Order, was denoted. He was the head of the Goliardic family, the Primate of the Wandering Students' Order, the

---

[1] See Novati, *Carmina Meaii Aevi*, p. 8, note.
[2] *Decameron*, i. 7.　　　　[3] See above, p. 25.
　　　[4] Grimm, op. cit., p. 189 et seq.

Archpoet of these lettered minstrels. The rare excellence of the compositions ascribed to him caused them to be spread abroad, multiplied, and imitated in such fashion that it is now impossible to feel any certainty about the personality which underlay these titles.

Though we seem frequently upon the point of touching the real man, he constantly eludes our grasp. Who he was, whether he was one or many, remains a mystery. Whether the poems which bear one or other of his changing titles were really the work of a single writer, is also a matter for fruitless conjecture. We may take it for granted that he was not Walter Map; for Map was not a Canon of Cologne, not a follower of Reinald von Dassel, not a mark for the severe scorn of Giraldus. Similar reasoning renders it more than improbable that the Golias of Giraldus, the Primas of Salimbene, and the petitioner to Reinald should have been Walter of Lille.[1]

At the same time it is singular that the name of Walter should twice occur in Goliardic poems of a good period. One of these is the famous and beautiful lament :—

[1] Giesebrecht identifies Walter of Lille with the Archipoeta. But he seems to be unacquainted with Salimbene's Chronicle, and I agree with Hubatsch that he has not made out his point.

"Versa est in luctum—cithara Waltheri."

This exists in the MS. of the *Carmina Burana,* but not in the Paris MS. of Walter's poems edited by Müldner. It contains allusions to the poet's ejection from his place in the Church—a misfortune which actually befell Walter of Lille. Grimm has printed another poem, *Saepe de miseria,* in which the name of Walter occurs.[1] It is introduced thus :

"Hoc Gualtherus sub-prior
Jubet in decretis."

Are we to infer from the designation *Sub-prior* that the Walter of this poem held a post in the Order inferior to that of the Primas ?

It is of importance in this connection to bear in mind that five of the poems attributed in English MSS. to Golias and Walter Map, namely, *Missus sum in vineam, Multiformis hominum, Fallax est et mobilis, A tauro torrida, Heliconis rivulo, Tanto viro locuturi,* among which is the famous Apocalypse ascribed by Salimbene to Primas, are given to Walter of Lille in the Paris MS. edited by Müldner.[2] They are distinguished by a marked unity of style ; and what is also significant, a

[1] Op. cit., p. 235, also in *Carm. Bur.,* p. 74.
[2] Hannover, 1859.

lyric in this Paris MS., *Dum Gualterus aegrotaret*, introduces the poet's name in the same way as the *Versa est in luctum* of the *Carmina Burana*. Therefore, without identifying Walter of Lille with the Primas, Archipoeta, and Golias, we must allow that his place in Goliardic literature is very considerable. But I am inclined to think that the weight of evidence favours chiefly the ascription of serious and satiric pieces to his pen. It is probable that the Archipoeta, the follower of Reinald von Dassel, the man who composed the most vigorous Goliardic poem we possess, and gave the impulse of his genius to that style of writing, was not the Walter of the *Versa est in luctum* or of *Dum Gualterus aegrotaret*. That Walter must have been somewhat his junior ; and it is not unreasonable to assume that he was Walter of Lille, who may perhaps be further identified with the *Gualtherus sub-prior* of the poem on the author's poverty. This Walter's Latin designation, *Gualtherus de Insula*, helps, as I have observed above,[1] to explain the attribution of the Goliardic poems in general to Walter Map by English scribes of the fifteenth century.

After all, it is safer to indulge in no constructive speculations where the matter of inquiry is both vague and meagre. One thing appears tolerably manifest ;

[1] Page 27.

that many hands of very various dexterity contributed
to form the whole body of songs which we call
Goliardic. It is also clear that the Clerici Vagi
considered themselves a confraternity, and that they
burlesqued the institutions of a religious order, pretend-
ing to honour and obey a primate or bishop, to whom
the nickname of Golias was given at the period in which
they flourished most. Viewed in his literary capacity,
this chief was further designated as the Archpoet. Of
his personality we know as little as we do of that of
Homer.

BOOKS ON GOLIARDIC LITERATURE

Carmina Burana. Stuttgart. 1847.

Thomas Wright. The Latin Poems commonly attributed to Walter Mapes. Camden Society. 1841.

—— Anecdota Literaria. London. 1844.

—— Early Mysteries, etc. London. 1844.

Edélstand du Méril. Poésies Populaires Latines Antérieures au Douzième Siècle. Paris. 1843.

—— Poésies Populaires Latines du Moyen Age. Paris. 1847. ——

—— Poésies Inédites du Moyen Age. Paris. 1854.

Jacob Grimm. Gedichte des Mittelalters auf König Friedrich I., den Staufer. Berlin. 1843.

H. Hagen. Carmina Medii Aevi Max. Part. Inedita. Bern. 1877.

F. Novati. Carmina Medii Aevi. Firenze. 1883.

Mone. Anzeiger, vii.

W. Müldener. Die Zehn Gedichte von Walther von Lille. Hannover. 1859.

Champollion-Figeac. Hilarii Versus et Ludi. Paris. 1838.

Gaudeamus. Leipzig. 1879.

Carmina Clericorum. Heilbronn. 1880.

A. P. Von Bärnstein. Carmina Burana Selecta. 1880.

—— Ubi sunt qui ante nos? Würtzburg. 1881.

Giesebrecht. Die Vaganten. Allg. Monatscrift für W. und K. 1853.

O. Hubatsch. Die Lateinischen Vagantenlieder. Görlitz. 1870.

A. Bartoli. I Precursori del Rinascimento. Firenze. 1876.

Allgemeines Deutsches Commersbuch.

TABLE OF SONGS TRANSLATED IN THIS VOLUME

N.B.—In order to facilitate the comparison between my translations and the originals, I have made the following table. The first column gives the number of the song and the second the page in this book; the third column gives the beginning of each song in English; the fourth gives the beginning of each song in Latin. The references in the fifth column are to the little anthology called *Gaudeamus* (Leipzig, Teubner, 1879); those in the sixth column are to the printed edition of the Benedictbeuern Codex, which goes by the title of *Carmina Burana* (Stuttgart, auf Kosten des Literarischen Vereins, Hering & Co. printers, 1847).

No.	Page.	English.	Latin.	Gaud.	Car. Bur.
				Page.	Page.
1	50	At the mandate	Cum in orbem	3	251
2	56	Once, it was	Olim nostrum	6	...
3	59	I, a wandering	Exul ego	178	50
4	61	We in our	Nos vagabunduli	195	...
5	65	Boiling in my	Aestuans	34	67
6	75	Spring is coming	Ver redit	88	178
7	76	These hours of	Tempus est	100	211
8	78	Take your pleasure	Congaudentes	90	166
9	79	Winter's untruth	Vetus error	86	...
10	80	Winter, now	Cedit hiems	85	177
11	81	Now the fields	Jamjam virent	89	184
12	82	Spring returns	Ecce gratum	84	183
13	84	Vernal hours	Vernum tempus	81	...
14	85	Hail thou	Salve ver	...	193
15	88	Summer sweet	Dum aestas	97	196
16	89	The blithe young year	Anni novi	...	145
17	90	Now the sun	Omnia sol	109	177
18	92	In the spring	Veris dulcis	...	195
19	93	With so sweet	De pollicito	103	206
20	94	Wide the lime-tree	Late pandit	...	185
21	95	Yonder choir of	Ecce chorus	...	118
22	97	Meadows bloom	Virent prata	98	189

TABLE OF SONGS—*continued*

* The original of this song will be found in Geiger, *Humanismus und Renaissance*, p. 414.

† The original will be found in Moll, *Hymnarium*, p. 138.

Printed in Great Britain by Butler & Tanner Ltd., Frome and London